Raised a Hindu, Manoj ⬚
He worked as a teacher ⬚
First at the Edinburgh ⬚
and his wife won a BAI ⬚ ... ⬚ Christian, he continues
to work in property and runs Instant Apostle publishing
house and the faith-based South Asian Forum team of the
UK Evangelical Alliance.

"Behind its intentionally outrageous title, Manoj gives us a compelling, fast-moving, inspiring, and enjoyable read. It is a moving and much-needed account of God's ways with people from migrant Asian backgrounds."
Steve Bell, author, trainer, and Director of Interserve

"Manoj Raithatha has a fascinating story dealing with wealth, poverty, faith, and leadership. He tells his story with honesty and skill, and is a voice well worth listening to."
Revd Dr Graham Tomlin, Dean, St Mellitus College

"Manoj has become not only a colleague but a friend. Filthy Rich provides us with an amazingly encouraging account of a life turned around by a powerful encounter with Jesus. This is a book to read and enjoy but then to give away to a friend or neighbour and pray it will impact them."
Steve Clifford, General Director, Evangelical Alliance

"I have found this story to be both gripping and emotionally moving. It's a no-holds-barred account of the power of the cross to save and restore. I couldn't put the book down once I started it. A great resource tool for those who have no faith, those exploring a deeper meaning to life, and even longstanding believers. I will be recommending it to many Christian business people I know and giving it as a gift to those who are not yet followers of Christ. This is a true rags-to-riches, to true riches story!"
Steve Uppal, senior leader, All Nations Christian Centre, Wolverhampton

FILTHY RICH

The property tycoon who
struck real gold

Manoj Raithatha

MONARCH
BOOKS

Oxford UK, and Grand Rapids, USA

Published by Monarch Books
an imprint of
Lion Hudson plc
Wilkinson House, Jordan Hill Road,
Oxford OX2 8DR, England
Email: monarch@lionhudson.com
www.lionhudson.com/monarch

ISBN 978 0 85721 590 1
e-ISBN 978 0 85721 591 8

First edition 2015

Acknowledgments

Scripture quotations are from The Holy Bible, English Standard Version®
(ESV®) copyright © 2001 by Crossway, a publishing ministry of Good News
Publishers. All rights reserved.
Scripture quotations marked NIV taken from the Holy Bible, New
International Version, copyright © 1973, 1978, 1984 International Bible
Society. Used by permission of Hodder & Stoughton, a member of the
Hodder Headline Group. All rights reserved. 'NIV' is a trademark of
International Bible Society. UK trademark number 1448790.
Scripture taken from the New Century Version. Copyright © by Thomas
Nelson, Inc. Used by permission. All rights reserved.

A catalogue record for this book is available from the British Library

Printed and bound in the UK, January 2015, LH26

Some names in this book have been changed for the sake of anonymity.

To my wife, Maria, whom I failed many times. I am so sorry that it took me so long to appreciate the gift you are in my life.

To God, who loves me unconditionally and never gave up on me. To You belongs all the glory!

Contents

Acknowledgments

I want to give my heartfelt thanks to a number of people who have helped in making this book possible.

First of all, I want to thank my family for giving me the time and space to write it. I couldn't have completed my story without your immense understanding and love. Maria, thank you for all your encouragement and taking the time to read umpteen drafts of this book. Thank you also to my beautiful children, Chandni and Ishaan, for shaping my life, and for all the laughter you bring into our crazy home.

To my mother, Saroj, and my father, Mahendra, for allowing me to express my story with such honesty. Thank you for your continued support, generosity, and love over the years. In both of you, I have truly great parents.

Thank you, Georgina, for being the best mother-in-law a man could have. I keep on telling people there's none better! Thank you for helping me to grow spiritually and feeding me up on all those delightful roast dinners.

I also want to say a huge thank you to those of you who have impacted my life and thus my story. Sadly, I can't mention you all because there are so many of you, but please know that your kindness has not gone unnoticed. Thank you, Mr Massie-Blomfield, Marci Kristof, and Priya for taking the time to write your reflections at different points in my life story. I am thrilled that your words are in this book! I will be forever grateful to you, Mr Massie-Blomfield, for planting a "seed" in my life, and Marci Kristof, for watering and tending to it.

My sincere thanks also go to Ram Gidoomal and Peter Day for the instrumental part they have played in my faith journey. Thank you so much for your patient guidance and prayer support over the years.

This book has involved a number of people who have helped in shaping the final version. Thank you, Nige Freeman, Robin Thomson, and Clive Thorne for all your wise comments. You guys are awesome; to you I owe some serious appreciation.

Finally, I want to express my deep gratitude to Tony Collins, Jenny Ward, Sheila Jacobs, Margaret Milton, Roger Chouler and the team at Lion Hudson for giving me the opportunity to put pen to paper. Thank you for believing in the message of this book and for your continued encouragement. I am delighted to be working with such a wonderful group of people.

My spirit is lifted by the kindness of you all. Thank you for all you are and all you do.

Show me, Lord, my life's end
and the number of my days;
let me know how fleeting my life is.
You have made my days a mere handbreadth;
the span of my years is as nothing before you.
Everyone's is but a breath,
even those who seem secure.
Surely everyone goes around like a mere phantom;
in vain they rush about, heaping up wealth
without knowing whose it will finally be.

Psalm 39:4–6, NIV

1

Selling Sand

F ilthy rich! That's how rich I wanted to be. What was the point in being "just rich", when you could aspire to own the stars! I'm not talking about a few nice motors on the front driveway. I'm talking the full monty: private jet, lush apartment in New York, mansion in the country, and enough staff to cater for my every whim. Oh, and a sushi chef for my refined palate and expensive tastes. I wanted it all. I wanted to be "filthy rich". If gold itself could have been made to ooze out of my pores I'd have been the first to find out how.

Being rich meant more to me than having a tidy bank balance. It was about what money had to offer; there was status and recognition for sure, but above all, it would give me power. Power to do what I wanted and get what I wanted. When I was younger I recall being told about a very wealthy man we knew who had made his money in an unscrupulous fashion. Behind his back there were mutterings, but when his family suddenly appeared one day at a function they were treated like royalty. You see, at the end of the day money trumps morals; money equals power.

And yet, years later, standing on a stunning beach in Mauritius with my family, I felt I had anything but power. Cooped up on a private island in paradise meant I was losing money every second; I could almost see the pound signs going into the ether, washed away in the surf. Don't get me wrong, I had a forgiving wife and kids to die for. But in truth, once I had spent a few days doing the family thing I was ready to get back to my first love and the source of my wealth: property.

In the gleaming sun I was getting restless. The missus loved strolling along the beach. This was her thing, the sun on her back, lost in the beauty of the expansive blue ocean, picking up shiny pebbles and imagining how many years they had been around for. For Maria, the beach was where she felt connected to a grander purpose. She never said it, but I could see it in the way she would stand on the sands peacefully gazing for what seemed like hours into thin air.

As far as I was concerned, once you'd seen it, you'd seen it. And if you really wanted to see it again you could always take a photo of it. I remember when my twin sister, Meera, went to Malaysia and I had to sit through several reels of film that she had taken. Of course, I smiled and looked interested; that is, until we got to the sequence of pictures capturing a sunset over a thirty-minute time span. Now, that was excruciating. What a waste – just the scenery and no people in it. I mean, what craziness was that?

While Maria hankered after the sun, I always went for the shade. It made no sense at all. One half of the world wanted to be lighter and the other darker. At least here in the shade I could do some thinking about my property business. I was sure going to make the most of the few days I had left. Finding a tatty piece of paper, I began pulling together an expansion strategy – new divisions, three-year sale projections, calculations on how many years to make it into the Rich List – not forgetting corporate responsibility and all that jazz. There was no way I was going to be selfish with my money. I'd do my bit for the odd good cause and reap the adulation when people found out it was Mr so-and-so who gave the big fat donation.

I had found my own little study on this beautiful beach. I had finally arrived! This wasn't so bad after all: a comfy beach chair, someone to wipe my glasses when they got misty, and an ice-cold beer to quench my thirst. My own private island. Now, that was a thought, but only if you could sell the sand. After all, I was here to make money, not build sandcastles.

2

Early Days

I f my early life was a colour, it would have been beige. Not interesting enough to be brown or daring enough to be grey. Watford in the seventies was just beige.

Meera, my twin sister, and I lived in a small terraced house with our parents. Having been dragged out by the doctors ahead of my sister, this unquestionably granted me the position of "lord and master" over her. My line of persuasion was that in Indian culture the eldest was to be revered, dare I say worshipped... But in reality my attempts were all in vain. I may have been the elder twin, but it was clear to all from the outset that Meera was the natural leader. Not only was she beautiful and charming, but also far more intelligent than I could ever be.

When we were sent to our local primary school it took me a while to adjust, as at first I was unwilling to speak. For a while I had been happy for Meera to speak on my behalf, and anyway, whatever I thought sounded much better coming from her. I wasn't deemed intelligent enough to be jealous. When the words finally did start to arrive they didn't come easily – I just didn't feel comfortable in my own skin, and even as a kid, speaking to others just seemed to make this more obvious. Years later I would regularly sit down and watch a TV singing programme called *The Voice*, and at times be moved to tears by the unique talents of the contestants. It only recently dawned upon me why I was so enraptured by this programme – this was people expressing their voice, and I had spent my early childhood devoid of one.

Amidst the beige of growing up in Watford, there were fleeting moments of colour. There was the occasional family house party blaring out Abba with one of my married uncles trying to flirt with my mother. And then there was good old Lincolnshire (and I am not talking sausage). The thing is, even if we wanted to get out of caravanning we couldn't. My drop-dead gorgeous aunt would occasionally come with us. On the last day of our holiday a beauty contest would be held and she would win not just the competition but, you've guessed right, another caravan holiday. My parents could have chosen anywhere in the world, but we always ended up in some rain-sodden field.

And then there was our occasional meal at Chix Chox. It's interesting, isn't it, what facts we remember about our respective histories? For some it would be meaningful relationships, for others visiting exciting places, but for me it was eating mouthwatering deep fried chicken 'n' chips at Chix Chox. The taste was sumptuous, but without fail each time we went, my sister and I would be given just the one chicken leg each. Whoever heard of a one-footed chicken? But my parents were having none of it.

Some years later, I would come across a book which I would read to my kids about Marvin the sheep. He was always after a little bit more and before he knew it he had moved from a few blades of grass to devouring fields, countries, continents, and finally, the world. Left rather lonely and feeling a tad sick, Marvin proceeds to puke it all out, returning the world back to its former state – fields, sheep and all. Marvin was now back with his friends and much happier. The problem was, unlike Marvin, I felt I never had that little bit more as a kid, and deep down I sure wanted a taste of it. (For those of you who would like to read the book, it is *Marvin Wanted More!* by Joseph Theobald.)

But "excess" was not something the Raithatha family did. This restrained attitude to life clearly had a lot to do with my family history. Coming from a line of economic migrants, we were part of a chain of Indians who had moved to East Africa and subsequently to the UK in search of work and financial stability. During World War Two, my grandfather Govindji had made a load of money by briefly returning to India and exporting fabrics and blankets back to Kenya. Other business ventures would follow in sisal fibre, land, and property. Govindji had begun his entrepreneurial career supporting his father in their small grocery shop in Mombasa, and one day the expectations would be on my father to also support his parent. But first he was to be educated, and in 1959 my father, Mahendra, was sent to the UK to further his studies in civil engineering.

Mahendra's initial year in the UK went smoothly enough. But with emerging financial issues in Kenya, my father's yearly allowance soon began to dry up. Govindji was a huge risk-taker. He pursued a "live or let die" attitude. Being with him was like being on a terrifying roller coaster; there were the highs of excess and the deep lows of financial insecurity. This latest bout caused huge strain for my father as he tried to complete his studies and look after his younger brother who had followed him to the UK. With no real family to turn to in the UK, Mahendra struggled through for a number of years.

As for my mother, Sarojini, she came to the UK from Uganda in 1970 after her arranged marriage to my father. The whole of her family would follow two years later as refugees after the expulsion of the Asian community from Uganda by Idi Amin. For a while her parents and four sisters would remain with our parents as they took stock of having lost in an instant their home, business, and possessions. They had arrived with nothing more than the clothes on their backs. The comfortable existence they had created in Uganda was suddenly swept away and they would have to take up the arduous task of beginning from scratch. They may have come as refugees, but they would do all in their power to win back every last penny they had lost. Unsurprisingly, creating financial security would become an obsession for many within the East African Asian community. And so, like many other East African Asians, my father and mother quickly programmed themselves into working hard and building a nest egg. It would become their mantra as my father pursued a career as a civil engineer and my mother chipped in with various part-time jobs.

But despite living in a different country, my father still felt he was pursuing the life his parents wanted for him. My father had been brought up in a house of dominant "alpha" characters. Any drive or will to buck the status quo was slowly squeezed out of him. He was like the kid in the film *Dead Poets Society* who wanted to be on stage but his father refused to let him do so. I have no idea what my father wanted to be, I just don't think he was allowed the opportunity to work this out. His dad had good intentions, but Mahendra's life had already been mapped out for him: civil engineering, arranged marriage, supporting the family business. He was part of a big family where individuality was the cardinal sin.

However, an outlet from Mahendra's somewhat constrained life would come from an unlikely source. As a child, my father would frequently visit the Hindu temple. After his arranged marriage to my mother, he had installed a small temple in our house with little statues representing the various Indian deities. His fascination with spirituality grew as he watched the weekly Sunday church service on TV. But it was the Hare Krishna movement that was to really grab his attention. In the sixties and seventies it became a huge movement, with references appearing in several pop songs. The Beatles had been fascinated by this, and nearby in Aldenham, George Harrison had gifted a house to the cause. In 1973 at this very temple my father met A. C. Bhaktivedanta Swami Prabhupada, founder of the International Society for Krishna Consciousness. Prabhupada had committed himself to spreading the movement in the West, and my father was thrilled to have had the privilege to meet the spiritual leader in person. That single meeting was to have profound significance. Mahendra was captivated by the movement's message of chanting the Hare Krishna mantra to cleanse the heart, free oneself from past karma – actions in a previous life affecting a person's present life – and bring liberation.

My father was both a quiet and private man. He never spoke much about his past or his feelings but here, for the first time, at the temple, he was able to express himself with like-minded people. Following the Hindu deity Krishna would give Mahendra a new identity, helping him deal with life and providing a safe place to exist. For Mahendra, the aim of Hinduism was to escape the materialism of this world and the reincarnation cycle to reach *moksha*, "oneness with god". Religion pointed to another world, a better world, and in his eyes this was most certainly an attractive proposition. In the years that were to come, rising early and chanting for up to five hours a day would help my father get through the many family difficulties that would come his way, difficulties that really began with the recession of the early eighties.

When this economic crisis kicked in, the rhythm of our family life was suddenly disrupted. With unemployment pushing over 3 million, my father found himself to be one of those thrown on the rubbish heap. Despite a period of uncertainty, he eventually struck lucky and was offered a promising engineering position in a local company. However, in spite of this opportunity, my father surprisingly opted to join his elder brother in the family construction and swimming pool business in Nairobi, Kenya. They needed his help, and in the Asian community, when family call, you go. My grandfather had died a few years prior to this, but his presence had certainly not disappeared. It had been his desire that his sons would one day work together, and my father was not about to let Govindji's dream perish. Mahendra did what any dutiful son would do, and in 1981 the Raithatha household uprooted to start a new life in East Africa.

3

Toto, I Don't Think We're in Watford Any More

I n *The Wizard of Oz*, Dorothy leaves her black-and-white life and is confronted by the technicolour beauty of her new world. That was Kenya for me, a place that would forever change my life.

Excited about the prospect of moving, I had put on my Sunday best of blue cords and shirt for the trip. But any excitement at moving to Africa dissipated when I got on the plane. Being my usual curious self, I had reached out to look in the seat pocket and proceeded to pick up a bulging sick bag, the entire contents of which then emptied on my lap. Why on earth there was a full sick bag on a new flight I will never know. But no amount of outrage was going to change the fact that I was covered in someone else's vomit without a change of clothes. This was going to be a long eight-hour flight! Over thirty years later, I was reminded of this moment but with fresh perspective. It doesn't matter how clean we try to make ourselves, we will always be besmirched in some way.

But any frustration caused on the plane journey instantly evaporated when we landed in Kenya. I was hit by the sudden sensory overload of the sun, heat, and smells. I recall seeing the differing worlds of the rich with their grand houses and the poor in their tiny wooden shacks protected from the rain by corrugated metal roofs. That first night I remember lying wide awake, something I had never done before. This was the first night in an exciting new chapter of my life. Arriving had felt hugely significant, like destiny had brought me to these shores. I had no idea what the future would hold but I knew we were meant to be here, and that whatever unfolded, whether good or bad, was all part of the course.

Along with my sister, we were instantly enrolled at Cavina, a Christian school run by Mr and Mrs Massie-Blomfield. Under their charismatic leadership, I encountered a friendly atmosphere where learning was taken seriously. Wearing beautifully turned-out uniforms, here the children were expected to politely greet the teachers on their way to class. Along with learning Latin and Roman history, I was encouraged to play rugby and hockey, and participate in debating classes. This was a huge contrast to the schooling I had encountered back in England.

At first I attempted to hide behind my sister's success. While Meera continued to take pole position, I was quietly heading up the stragglers. Still, she always encouraged me with comforting words when I came seventeenth in the class. Of course, she downplayed the fact that there were only nineteen children in the form. Meera was an all-rounder, combining academic success with ballet and acting skills. My family still speak about her breathtaking lead performance as Dorothy in *The Wizard of Oz*. What role was I playing, you may wonder? Well, again, I was supporting my twin – this time as "soldier". OK, so it wasn't a speaking part... my five seconds on stage were there purely to make Meera look good!

Yet Cavina was not a school where you could hide for too long. With small classes and an emphasis on perseverance – the school motto being "Fortune Favours the Brave" – this was no place for wallflowers. This was a school in which everyone counted. Left with little choice, I reluctantly took the decisive step to engage in school life. I was never going to be super-bright but I did manage to slowly move up the rankings. More importantly, however, the school gave me a self-belief that I had never experienced before – for the first time I felt that I could be someone. These were strange stirrings and with these feelings came a sudden interest in Christianity.

Having regularly visited the Hare Krishna temple when I was back in England, the concept of religion was something I had grown up with. This had been at my father's instigation, but my mother too had an incredible faith in God. Unlike my father, she didn't speak much about it, always saying simply that God was within her and guiding her. Sarojini didn't buy into feeling compelled to regularly perform rituals or live a particular lifestyle to somehow be accepted by God. In many ways my father and mother's outlook on growing spiritually differed greatly – for him it involved structure and routine, while for her it was more free-flowing and emotive. The fact that I was living in a deeply spiritual home was further underlined each year when the whole family would go to the nine-day-long Navratri Hindu festival. This festival is dedicated to Durga, the mother goddess who represents power. It was a celebration of good triumphing over evil and was hugely important to my mother. She would regularly dedicate this period to fasting, praying, and drawing close to the particular deities she worshipped. Almost every year towards the end of the nine-day festival of dance, my mother would have an experience of some sort which would briefly change her countenance and leave her utterly exhausted as she connected with something from the spirit world. Each time this happened it would be followed by people surrounding my mother, wishing to pay their respects to a woman they believed had encountered the divine. No one ever explained to me what was going on, but as a youngster I felt that in some way I was part of a uniquely spiritual family for whom God was profoundly important. I would have liked to have asked my mother what happened during those moments, but somehow it never felt right to do so.

So, growing up in such an environment quickly opened me up to the importance of having a faith. Despite the fact I would have described myself as a Hindu, I found myself fascinated and profoundly moved by the Christian belief that God humbled Himself by taking on human flesh and dying on a cross to save humanity. From my perspective, the cross sounded like the craziest act I had ever heard of. I mean, why would a creator die for the created? This was certainly a very different kind of God to the Hindu deities I knew of.

Christianity was a part of the school's daily life, from whole school hymn-singing to optional lunchtime Bible study. It wasn't an added extra but part of the school's very DNA. Interestingly, as the months rolled by, I found myself openly talking about God and once even plucked up the courage to galvanize my hockey teammates to pray at the half-time whistle. I remember the moment clearly – we were being thrashed 4–0 and I felt a sudden urge to pray! I took a moment to look around at all my teammates. Was I crazy? With my reputation on the line, I gathered everyone together and watched in wonder as one by one, without any challenge or even a smirk, my teammates fell to their knees and closed their eyes. That moment was sensational; the noise around us suddenly disappeared and all that was left were my words as I led the team in a simple earnest prayer for help.

At the final whistle, we still ended up losing the game, but less embarrassingly at 4–3. No doubt, in another school, asking a group of lads with hockey sticks to pray might have resulted in me taking a beating and a trip to the local hospital. But from that simple encounter, I realized that there had to be a greater force out there. There was simply no way we could have got three goals in the second half. The school house I belonged to was utterly useless at sports – we never won anything, and in all honesty we should have been thrashed by a few more goals. We had tried God and He seemed to have come through for us, maybe not to win the game but at least to see us make a good fightback.

At home, my interest in Christianity was to manifest itself in debating religion with my father. I was convinced there was something in this Jesus character. I could see it in the way Mr Massie-Blomfield talked about God, like he knew Him personally, like they were the closest of friends. I could see it in his eyes when he sang with passion the school hymns of God's sacrifice. This was more than superficial ritual; something deep was going on in that man's heart every time he mentioned the name of Jesus. But my father was quick to counter my arguments, asserting the superiority of Hinduism as the ultimate path to God. In essence, the focus of both faiths was achieving salvation and eradicating the sin which stood in the way, but they had irreconcilable answers to the same problem. For my father, this was achievable by our efforts, but for the

Christian it was not achieved by one's own doing but by God Himself paying the price for our sin through Jesus' death on the cross. The argument was between one of our "works" versus God's "grace" – His free gift – and neither of us was prepared to concede defeat.

The Krishna religion had become very important to my father, and as a parent now myself, I understand just how hard it can be to find your children questioning something that is so central to your identity. When our debates began to grow more intense, my father moved the family temple into my bedroom. I have vivid memories of my father for a while coming into my room at 5:30 each morning, switching the lights on full, and proceeding to chant aloud. Anyone who knows my father would describe him as a quiet and peaceful man, yet in this question of religion I had somehow touched something in him that was phenomenally passionate.

In reality, my father had to do very little to curb my interest in Christianity as it gradually waned of its own accord when I moved on to secondary school. And as it waned, life inevitably was not the same. Cavina School had made me feel alive; it had given me my voice. Here I had felt the presence of something greater, something grander, and for five years I had breathed in this new air. When I left, the presence lingered for a while but then one day, without warning, it just went – just like that.

At secondary school, other interests began to take priority. Unbeknown to me, a small enterprising seed was germinating within me. Here in Nairobi I was fed the tales of my grandfather's rise to riches. He had built an entire office block in Nairobi, but had lost countless money in "get rich quick" schemes; it was hard to find an Asian businessman who did not know his name. He had flaunted his wealth and didn't care which feathers he ruffled. He was even brazen enough to buy a large house opposite the British High Commission. What was there not to like about him? I wanted to be just as audacious and successful, and this desire was further fuelled by our current predicament.

At first, life in Nairobi had been great. After all, we were living in my uncle's splendid five-bedroom house with its own driveway and extensive gardens. But within months, the relationship between my uncle and my father became fraught with tension. On the surface we were living the good life. But the daily reality was not knowing when the next pay cheque would come, and although they were brothers, for some reason my father and uncle couldn't get along with each other.

Despite the difficult situation we found ourselves in, my incredibly inventive mother quickly set about transforming the family kitchen into a small business, baking and selling cakes. There was no way my mother was going to see her children go hungry. As a child, I was aware of the reality of the situation. Yet whenever I was granted permission to lick the leftovers from the mixing bowl, I could drift far away into a world devoid of problems. To this day, my mother still makes the best chocolate gateau!

Determination was definitely in my mother's bloodstream. As one of six strong-willed sisters sharing just one bedroom in their home in Kampala, she quickly learnt to look after herself. However, the most notable influence on her life was Girdhardas, her late father. He was a kind, generous and loving man who raised his family to respect and value each other. Through running the family crockery business, he was able to provide maybe not a luxurious lifestyle, but certainly enough for the family to live. As a child, my mother took every opportunity to be around the man she so clearly admired, and while her sisters were busy being teenagers, my mother loved to sit in the family shop and help her father with the bookkeeping and cashing up at the end of the day. But more than anything else, this was an opportunity to listen to a man with endless stories and lessons on how to get through the trials and tribulations that spring up from time to time in the course of life.

Girdhardas certainly knew a thing or two about this. With the loss of his own father at the age of nine, he had been forced to look after both his mother and sisters, and at the tender age of twelve he had made the trip from India to Africa as he struggled to earn money to support his family. Maybe he had an intuitive sense that his daughter would require wisdom in the years to come. Like any good father, he did what he felt was right for his daughters. And it was in this spirit that he believed he did the right thing when he did not let my mother continue her studies, but instead arranged her marriage to my father. Most certainly, this proved to be extremely challenging for my mother, but to this day I have never heard her say anything negative about the decisions her father took. In all of this, her experiences shaped her into the woman she is today.

As I observed the tensions at home, my thoughts turned to making money. I was committed to not making the same mistakes as my father, who was reliant on his brother for his weekly pay packet. One day I would be my own boss and be in control of my own destiny. With this in mind, I studied accounts in secondary school and put what I learnt in the classroom to "good use". I began selling alcohol and cigars in school, "under the radar". However, this business venture was short-lived when one of my fellow students drew attention to it by throwing an empty bottle of alcohol out of the school bus window. Fortunately, no one was hurt.

Despite the sudden closure to my miniature business, I had had my first taste of making money. And the taste was good. Christianity had been a nice idea, but what did that have to do with the cut and thrust of living in the real world where my parents were struggling to make ends meet? Cavina had taught me to believe in the impossible, to achieve the highest heights and come what may, I would hold on to the school motto of "Fortune Favours the Brave". But as for all that religious stuff, I firmly closed the door on that wacky phase of my life – there was no point in dwelling on it one minute longer. Suffice to say I had come through, and my father was most certainly relieved. I now turned my focus to the future; what I could become, what I could achieve. The adventure was only just starting.

4

Passion in Portsmouth,
Wanting in Watford

t was 1988, and I was sixteen years old. My parents
scraped together their hard-earned savings and
suddenly decided to send my sister and me back
to the UK; Meera went to London while I was put into a
Catholic boys' school in Portsmouth. It would come at a
heavy financial cost, but somehow they would find a way.
Our being sent back to the UK for school formed part of
our parents' decision to move back permanently. Kenya
had been a nightmare for them. Relationships with our
extended family had disintegrated and my father was
no longer working for his brother but scraping by on
odd jobs. My parents would follow us one year later,
once they had tied up loose ends.

I may have arrived as the "freshie" but I was no
longer the quiet, unassuming boy that had left England
all those years before. I had come back with a suitcase
full of self-belief and an unwavering confidence that I
was going to make something of my life. Kenya had been
key to my destiny, and now I had returned to put what
I had learnt into practice. Africa had given me a heart

for business, but if I was to really make it in this field, I would need more than a few catchy ideas. Enterprise involved relationships and I needed to learn to get on with people from all walks of life, and a Catholic boys' boarding school provided just the right playing field to hone my craft.

Arriving with a strong African accent wasn't the greatest start. I had to move fast to avoid bullying and being labelled as some weirdo. The ability to drink copious amounts of alcohol and smoke like a chimney quickly helped me fit in. As in any school there were many sects: the sporty, the popular, the geeks, the smokers. I had aligned with the latter. It was the easiest option. You offered out some cigarettes, you were accepted and became one of the boys. The smoke united us. It was hardly the challenge I was expecting. Having left the UK without a voice and come back with my own swagger, I sure wasn't going to allow myself to morph into some group identity. Fitting in was cool, getting alongside people was great, but retaining identity was paramount.

Being "generous" with my money would become my trump card. Buying rounds instantly earned me "friends", but more importantly, it won me recognition. Sure, I was still part of the pack, but now I was much more. Who wouldn't crave the attention? But there was a problem. I was pretty good when it came to figures but had got a tad carried away with the ride. I had been so efficient in generously blowing my money that I soon found myself having to work evenings as a cleaner in Woolworths to sustain my spending habits. Now that I had started, there was no going back. I loved spending and I hated those who didn't spend. You know the type – always slow in putting their hands in their wallets. You could see them a mile away; you'd be at the bar but they'd choose to stand a bit behind you and when it was time to cough up they would suddenly decide to engage in conversation with someone else. Annoyingly they'd always end with a sweet thank-you line: "Oh, cheers for the drinks."

There would always be the scroungers; that just came with the territory. But I allowed it, because I was learning so much, and you really couldn't put a price on that. Money had the potential to win people over. It had the ability to change circumstances. I was no longer on the periphery but had moved into the centre. And I discovered that it was from the centre that you could control the circle of life – both yours and others'.

What a revelation! It was so obvious, but it was only now as I was playing the generosity card that I began to truly appreciate the extent of the power of money to gain control. Money was a real-life magnet. There was no point in fighting it, because the lure was way too great. This was with teenagers, but it's as true with adults – years later at my children's school, I watched with interest as both the children and their parents gravitated to one family in particular that were exceedingly wealthy. It didn't matter what they were like – good or bad – people simply wanted to be around them. Over the course of a term, I saw how a group of seemingly kind and approachable parents morphed into utter aloofness and cold-heartedness as they moved out of the "uncool sect" of the less wealthy and into the main "A" group. The choice was simple – join or be forever ostracized. But what really got me was all this was happening without them having the faintest realization that money was subtly working away in their lives, transforming them and dominating their decision-making.

But it wasn't just my experiences outside of the classroom that were shaping my world perspective at Portsmouth. I was on the cusp of going to university and determined not to fall into some dead-end degree that would lead nowhere. Mr Thomas, my charismatic A-level English teacher, gave me more than I bargained for. He wanted all his students to be passionate for their subject. He never spelt it out. He never articulated it. He didn't need to. He lived it. He loved books and he loved teaching. Yes, he wanted his students to do well, but above all he wanted the students to catch a glimpse of the joy of having a deep and passionate interest. For Mr Thomas it was his passion to read and be lost in new worlds and new stories. This wasn't just some words on a piece of paper. This was his life. The question was, what was I truly passionate about?

Mr Thomas's philosophy made sense; I couldn't drift through life doing something I wasn't passionate about. As I read, I began to see what Mr Thomas meant. In James Joyce's *A Portrait of the Artist as a Young Man*, the main character, Stephen Dedalus, questions and rebels against the Catholic and Irish conventions under which he had grown up. I, too, needed the courage to question my life. In the poetry of Yeats I came face to face with the poet's passion for a woman – he didn't just love Maud Gonne, he passionately poured out his heart for her. His feelings were deep, delving way beyond the surface. Whatever I was going to do with my life, I needed to scratch deeper; I needed to be passionate. To be a phony would be the ultimate sin. I could make packets of money, but it would mean absolutely nothing if I wasn't passionate. Stephen Dedalus struggled in the first twenty years of his life. I guessed Mr Thomas had struggled too, and what he shared came from the experiences of a challenging life. I would be a fool not to heed his wisdom. Money was good – but what about passion?

A superficial connection with faith was re-established at St John's College in Portsmouth, but that didn't give me any answers. We used to go to Mass every Sunday but it was more bore than awe. The cross was there, but I no longer felt the presence. Maybe it was just me. Had I distanced myself from God? Or was that feeling of something transcendent that I had had at Cavina just all in my head? As I turned up every week to Mass, I increasingly found faith to be irrelevant. The Catholic brothers didn't talk about God in the same way as the Massie-Blomfields had in Kenya. Maybe the brothers' faith was a private affair. Or maybe "religion" had replaced "relationship".

And there would be no answers coming from home. My family had other things on their plate. After a decade of huge challenges, my parents returned to their little terraced home in Watford. I recall going back to our house that had been trashed by a series of tenants and being given the arduous task of cutting through the layers of fat that had built up over the years on the kitchen stove. Yet at least we had a roof over our heads and food on the table.

For my parents, the move back proved demanding, with nothing to show for the last ten years of their lives. Making material progress was and still is the primary goal of many within the Asian community, and sadly my parents were left despondent by their failure to have prospered as they had been expecting to. It was financial success that gave you recognition, and while our UK-based relatives were now living in bigger houses and running successful businesses, we were back where we had started a decade before. Why hadn't my parents cut their losses and come back earlier? Whatever their reasons for staying on in Kenya, the final straw had come when they ended up, along with my younger brother and sister, having to share one bedroom in another relative's house.

Unfortunately for my parents, life back in England was not going to get any easier. The stress of finding themselves unemployed, their previous job skills now redundant as they were passed over in favour of younger talent, finally took its toll on their marriage, along with everything else, and they separated. In hindsight, it probably shouldn't have happened, but the difficulties seemed insurmountable at the time – Kenya was a blast that had ripped a hole in the heart and soul of my parents' marriage, and they were in a dark place, their will and energy to hold things together completely broken.

The week before my mother finally left, she asked me to help move her belongings into a flat. She had wanted my dad to pick up the pieces and make a go of it. But my father's energy had been sapped and he was a broken man. I remember when she left that my father just sat there in the sitting room staring into the distance. Why didn't he run after her, why didn't he stop her, why didn't he plead with her to give it another go? If only he had said something, just maybe she would have come back.

Like many eighteen-year-olds at that time I found myself drawn to a new album called *Disintegration* by The Cure. It reflected the band's return to an introspective gothic rock style with increased pressure to create a more enduring work. And enduring it was. "Disintegration" remains The Cure's highest selling record to date, and their ultimate break-up song had come out in 1989, the year my parents split. The songs of this album gave me great comfort. I certainly wasn't the first to see their parents separate, and it had somehow become the norm in modern Britain. The thing is, this wasn't my parents' fault. They had committed to each other, they had adhered to their parents' wishes. They had made a good go of it and had gone to Kenya with all the right intentions. But not even their deep-rooted faith could hold it all together.

I thought I had taken my parents' separation in my stride. I thought I was all right, but on reflection I was hurting and somehow The Cure provided just the tonic to get me through the reality of our family breakdown. These things may have been common in much of Britain, but they didn't happen in the Asian community, where divorce was rare. You certainly didn't hang your washing out in public by divorcing – problems were supposed to remain hidden behind closed doors.

As the reality of my parents' separation sunk in, I found myself caught in the tension. I had always loved the idea of being my own boss and making money, and the impact of their split had taught me the importance of being self-reliant and financially secure. But Mr Thomas had also stirred a tempting alternative – to live passionately! I needed to find out what I was passionate about and how it would make me money. I had much thinking to do about the next stage of my life. I would get an opportunity much sooner than I expected.

5

Freedom Pass

My failure to get the grades to study economics at Bath was a huge blow. I recall slamming the front door behind me as I stormed out to get some fresh air. I thought I had done enough, but it was in English that I had excelled and not economics! Maybe this was meant to happen; maybe it was part of the course. Mr Thomas had come up trumps after all, and maybe three further years of studying economics would have been too much for me. What seemed at first to be the worst possible result suddenly became a lifeline. I had been so close to making a decision that could have ruined the rest of my life, but I now had a real chance to do something which excited me. However the only thing I could come up with was studying English. The clearing system conjured up Bangor University and so Bangor it was, though I would take a year out first.

My poor mum did not have time to disapprove when I told her I was going travelling. I had raised enough money, so when a close friend introduced me to three Canadians who were on their way to inter-railing around Europe I jumped at the chance to meet them.

During their stop in London I paid for dinner. My generosity paid off and forty-eight hours later I was on my way to France with my new friends. Our travelling together would only last about ten days. We had just arrived in Rome when I made the decision to go my separate way. It had been wonderful to be with them, but this sense had been brewing for a few days that I should go on alone, so before I could change my mind, we parted company. They quite rightly had specific plans about what to do and what to see, but I had an intuitive sense that for some reason this was not the course I was meant to follow.

My decision to travel on my own was totally surreal. I hadn't done anything like this before. On the face of it, there was no need to go alone. However, what I was increasingly realizing was that my life was not really my own. I didn't articulate it as such, but always felt that there was someone watching out for me and guiding my steps. Every now and then I would catch myself stopping to acknowledge this force that was out there. They were brief moments as I was always quick to brush them aside and get back to engaging with the "real world". I have no idea why I refused to rest in these reflective moments – but for whatever reason, I was always in a rush to block out any thoughts of God or a supernatural force. Here in Rome, however, away from my normal home and world, I had allowed the moment to linger, and that is when I knew I was being led to follow a different path.

As I left Rome, I felt liberated. What quickly became evident was that this was not simply going to be just a trip taking in a few sights or meeting a few people along the way – no, this would be a journey of grappling with the meaning of "freedom". This word had suddenly captivated my heart. I wanted freedom. Freedom from what, I had no idea. All I knew was that I wanted to feel it, to taste it, to own it. I wanted to peel away the layers from this word and find out what was at its core. What was it like to be truly free?

Whilst lying awake in my cousin's room when I had first arrived in Kenya, there was a moment when I felt this experience was going to be hugely significant. That was a moment in time when I was on my own and silent and it was in that quietness that I was able to hear. Some ten years had elapsed since then and here I was, an adult, in that place of solitude again. There were no audible voices; just a gentle nudge when it was time to move on as I travelled across Italy, Austria, Germany, and what was then Czechoslovakia. Though I was alone I never felt alone. It felt like I was on an assignment, each country taking me one step closer to finding out what this was all for.

And then it happened. I was in Denmark at some tourist site when I met Jorgen. He was actually from Canada, like my previous travelling partners, but with a completely different philosophy. There weren't any specific countries or tourist sites that he was hankering to see. For Jorgen, that would have been an imposition, hindering him from being led and spoken to by the land and by life. We immediately got on like old friends, and before I knew it he had taken out a map of Europe and tossed a coin over it to see where we should go. It landed on the South of France so that was where we headed. It made no sense for me to go there as I had already been there on my recent travels, but for some unknown reason it just felt right to go back – and with Jorgen it was sure to be different this time.

The next few weeks were hugely thought-provoking. Jorgen was unlike anyone else I knew. He loved the present moment and lived fully in it. I was constantly looking ahead, living for the future, whereas he was blissfully enjoying the here and now, savouring each and every breath. He later shared that he had been very ill with a brain tumour, but far from feeling sorry for himself he appeared to have accepted it as simply another part of his journey on earth. He seemed to be at rest with the fact that his life was fragile and that his time here could come to an end sooner rather than later. Despite the threat of his condition, he seemed free of its possible consequence. Not even the thought of death was holding him back. Unlike me, he wasn't carrying the chains of organizing, planning, controlling, discerning. He appeared to take one step at a time, refusing to allow logic to interrupt the flow, unfazed by what lay ahead. I was constantly planning my future, whereas he was allowing his future to come to him.

Cannes was great. Boy, was it worth it. It was worth it for a single moment on the beach when everything seemed to be perfect; when it didn't matter if I was going to be rich, it didn't matter what degree I was going to do, and it didn't matter what I was going to become. It was great for that single moment when all that mattered was the here and now, being on this stunning beach with the heat of the sun gently resting on my skin. In the peace of the moment I realized how exhausted I was by all the thinking my brain had been putting me through. In the letting go I began to experience a new kind of freedom. It seemed like all along the journey of life I had met interesting people that had had huge significance in my life – Mr Massie-Blomfield, Mr Thomas, and now Jorgen. Where was this all leading, I wondered? But to think on this would have been to try to take control, so I stopped.

When I came back to the UK I was a different man. I had Jorgen's address in Montreal and immediately booked a surprise visit. Within six weeks I had arrived on his doorstep. I met his friends, had great conversations, and we laughed. Jorgen loved the song "With or Without You" by U2 and I recall him singing the song as he played on his acoustic guitar. I can picture the moment so clearly, sitting on the balcony listening to him as he poured his heart out through the song. Like Bono, Jorgen seemed to be trying to reconcile some inner turmoil but, like Mr Thomas, he never shared what was going on in his head – there was always a mystery. Both he and Mr Thomas left me with a taste for a different way of looking at the world, and on recollection I can see why.

That was the last time I would ever see Jorgen. A few years later I would get a letter from his sister saying that he had passed away. I was shocked. Cancer had taken him. I had no idea how she had got my address. I called her and she spoke about how I was just one of many who had been deeply impacted by meeting her brother. His life had been relatively short, but its influence had been huge. What blew me away was that this man had been taken through the mill and somehow had got through the other side mentally unscathed. I think Jorgen had committed the rest of his life to making a difference by sharing his well thought-out philosophy of letting go and living freely for the moment.

A year or so before Jorgen died, my grandfather on my mother's side had passed away. I was in my final year at St John's in Portsmouth at the time, and this was the first funeral I had attended for a close family member. The open coffin had brought home to me the reality of death – and now Jorgen's death further compounded the realization that life was short and its end sudden.

On returning to my boarding house after my grandfather's funeral, I remember being awake in my room one night. My roommate was not around when suddenly my grandfather, Girdhardas, appeared in the right-hand corner of the room. I curled up in a ball, petrified, but he calmed me down and simply told me to look after his wife. That is all he said, and for days I wondered if this had been a dream, and if it hadn't been, then why had he visited me? I figured that he clearly knew something and for some reason he had been allowed to come to me. I can't say I did a good job of looking after my grandmother, but years later my grandfather's words would take on deeper significance. I know this seems a bizarre incident and some readers might think it sounds like spiritualism; but, I believe I really did see my grandfather.

So, death had become very real. Jorgen's parents had had to see their own son die, something that should never have been. The vision of seeing my grandfather pointed to something beyond. What was this life for, and what happened when we died? So many questions, and all this was pointing to God again.

6

How Far Could I Go?

t seemed like Kenya, boarding at St John's, and travelling were periods of preparation. But for what, I had no idea. I had learnt so much about the power of money, the importance of passion, and more recently the freedom that came with letting go. Arriving at university seemed like the penultimate step before all these experiences would come together and realize their fruit. It felt like my experiences were giving me options. There was business versus passion, control verses letting go. It appeared as if life had thrown up all these ideas and sometime soon I was finally going to have to decide which path I would choose to follow.

One area of my life that I suddenly felt compelled to make a decision on was the subject of faith in God. As I have mentioned, I had flirted with the idea of Christianity, but as I moved on to secondary school it had lost its appeal. Yet there was no denying the sense of a higher force on my travels around Europe. I hadn't been at university long before I was invited to a "charismatic" Christian church – I stood at the back of the church hall utterly astonished by what I was witnessing. Don't get me wrong, I had stepped into a church or two in my time, but what I wasn't prepared for was a room full of "happy clappers" belting out songs like they were on some A-class drugs. I just couldn't fathom why they were behaving so bizarrely. What was there to be happy about in singing a few songs to someone who wasn't even visibly present in the room? I was relieved when it was all over and I could make a quick exit from these weirdos who wore permanent smiles on their faces.

That day I turned my back again on this Christian God who seemed to have been following me around. It wasn't like I had made any commitment of faith to Him, so why couldn't He just leave me alone? Why couldn't He be like the Hindu deities that let me just be? As a youngster I had been frightened of the Hindu gods, but with age I had come to accept that this was my faith and no one was going to change my mind. I may not have visited the temple regularly or practised my Hindu faith as such, but it was a part of me and my upbringing. What's more, my Hindu faith didn't interfere with my life. After all, I had many reincarnation cycles to work my way out of the materialism of this world. I couldn't be doing with the urgency of Christianity, which demanded commitment and surrender in this life before we met our Maker face to face. Why surrender the various pleasures this world had to offer – especially right now when I had taken a particular liking to a young woman called Sarah? When it came to the subject of women, I can't say I was the most experienced. It seemed like everything happened so quickly in the UK whereas I was still some sad guy learning the ropes, and so it was hardly surprising that female attention was slow to come.

It didn't take me long to fall for Sarah. She was part of my friendship circle and I had liked her for weeks but didn't think I was her type. One evening she came to the student bar in a figure-hugging dress. I tried to make my move, but was immediately cut short by one of the athletic, canoeing types. You know the sort: tall, muscular, blond wavy hair – extremely annoying! Looking at my tired attire, I stood no chance. I wasn't one for giving up, but when I saw Sarah being playfully encouraged by Mr Canoe-man to sit on his lap, I quickly said my goodbyes. I had conceded defeat and carried my miserable self back to my room. There had been a number of girls I had liked over the years, but this one felt special, and I knew I had lost my chance. But then to my astonishment there was a knock on my door, and there was Sarah wanting to come in.

Within days I was in a seriously intense relationship. We became that irritating couple who were always together during term-time and holidays. It was an all-consuming affair of dramatic highs and lows which somehow lasted throughout the laughter and turmoil of university. I really couldn't imagine life without her, and assumed she felt the same.

We were quick to share a flat after university and I had soon followed my girlfriend into teaching. I didn't want to go down this career route – but then again, I hadn't the faintest idea what I wanted to do with my life and following her seemed the easiest thing. As for Sarah, she knew exactly what she wanted. She loved literature and poetry, and saw teaching as her destiny. I had done a great job derailing her plans during a year out following graduation, but now she was back on course to fulfilling her dreams and I was being dragged with her. It was all a blur. Did I fill in the PGCE application? I probably did – but with my girlfriend's help! I got accepted at Roehampton Institute and twelve months later I was being offered a job as an English teacher.

And then it happened. My girlfriend dropped the bombshell that she wanted out. It came totally out of the blue, at least for me! If there were any cracks I was either unaware of them or had subconsciously paved over them. Five years and it ended in an instant. I was utterly wrecked by the shock of it all as I tried to make sense of what was happening.

There was nothing I could do to change Sarah's mind. She wanted out and that was final – there was no time for questions. I recall the last time I saw her in Putney High Street as she walked away; I was never to see her again. I continued to stare, longing for her to come back, yet knowing she wouldn't and that she was leaving without any forwarding address or contact number.

For months I was boring everyone who came within an inch of me with my sob story. It would be a long time before I was able to pull myself together. Inspiration would come from a familiar source; if Jorgen had somehow managed to battle through life with a joyful spirit then so could I. After all, my problems were nothing compared to what he went through. As I began to work through the pain of separation and recall times with Jorgen and others, a sense of who I was and what I wanted to achieve began to re-emerge. Past experiences of Kenya, Cavina, Mr Thomas, and Jorgen had been locked away for the past five years with Sarah, but now they were being rediscovered. Accepting my new life without Sarah suddenly brought everything rushing back.

The process of sifting happened quickly. I had already done away with Christianity early on in my university life and I wasn't about to think of it again. Then there was the "Fortune Favours the Brave" motto. For some this was just some silly saying that you wore on your blazer, but it had revolutionized my outlook on life. Yes, I would take that and turn it into risk-taking. And then there was Mr Thomas and what he had taught me. I had allowed myself to drift through life unsure of what I wanted to do, and while I still wasn't sure, I certainly wasn't going to allow myself to accept the status quo any longer. And then there was business. My desire for making money was returning. For five years I had closed the door on key moments and influences from my past, almost forgetting that they even existed, but now, with sifting completed and God firmly sidelined, I was ready to take control of my destiny once more. Risk, passion, and determination were going to make a powerful cocktail.

Something deep within me had changed the day my girlfriend left. I had believed in the "happily ever after" story, but that had proved to be nothing but a lie. She had her reasons and I am sure they were valid, but the underlying hurt was there and would lead me down a destructive path for many years, as women simply became objects of desire as opposed to individuals with hearts and emotions. I could write a whole book about all those miserable experiences and the pain they caused, but suffice it to say, I messed up.

Evidently, a new man was emerging. There had been glimpses at St John's of what I could become before love for Sarah kicked the stuffing out of me. University had turned me into some soppy love-struck puppy dog and I hardly recognized the new Manoj that was now standing before me. I was ready for action, but first I would have to deal with this teaching dilemma!

Teaching had been Sarah's dream; not mine. But having accepted my first teaching post at a school in Sutton, I tried to make the most of it. For a while I even started dressing up in comfy cardigans to look like a bona fide English teacher. Who was I kidding? I couldn't even spell, my head of English kindly pointing out one day that "separate" had two "a"s and wasn't spelt "seperate". I may have had the gift of the gab but the truth of the matter was that my ex-girlfriend had got two degrees, hers and mine!

I had two options: get out, or gun for promotion. As I still had no clear inkling about what to do outside of teaching I tried the promotion route. Encouraged by a senior teacher, I put together a detailed document on setting up a gifted and talented programme in the school, only to find out once I had put in the hours that they weren't prepared to give me a pay rise the following year. I couldn't believe I had been taken for a ride, and within weeks I had handed in my notice and acquired a job heading up a new drama department in a secondary school in south London. It was no surprise I was moving into a different subject area. I couldn't understand long words. I hated intellectual conversation and having to pretend I understood witty jokes. My brain was just not wired that way. Give me a simple film with a progressive plotline any day of the week. Why was I trying to pretend to be something I wasn't cut out to be? The only consolation was that I wasn't like my colleague, who refused to mark his students' work, choosing instead to put the homework in a private box under his desk. At the end of the year he would bag it all up and dispose of it. How he got away with it I have no idea!

But even teaching in a new school didn't give me the sensation I was hankering after. Don't get me wrong there were some really great days, especially seeing the academically weaker students excel. But it just wasn't satisfying my soul. Yes, I had come in on a higher salary with responsibility, but I certainly wasn't prepared to play the waiting game to move further up the career ladder. If there had been a super-fast track option then maybe I could have been persuaded.

After just one year I handed in my notice and enrolled on a Masters' course in drama at Royal Holloway, University of London. At this point I may have appeared somewhat manic, chopping and changing my career at every opportunity. But now that Sarah was gone, there was absolutely nothing stopping me. I had wasted too much of my life drifting and I was living fearlessly as I sought that deep-rooted passion Mr Thomas had talked about. Handing in my notice certainly didn't go down well with a school that had recently appointed me to set up the drama department, but after the dust had settled they offered me a part-time consultancy position while I pursued further studies. Why an MA in drama? To put it simply, I fancied the idea of becoming a professional director. To some, such ideas may have seemed high and flighty. What they didn't know was that I had been schooled to believe in the impossible.

Every minute of the MA course would be invaluable if I was going to reach the dizzy heights of success. This wasn't simply about passing exams. This about grabbing every opportunity for a grander purpose and greater success. So when I got the opportunity to direct a thirty-minute piece, I got to work quickly. While my fellow students chose scenes from well-known play scripts, I rose to the challenge of writing and directing my own piece.

The short play was called *BBA and Proud* and charted the highs and lows of a group of British Asian friends. BBA stood for British-Born Asian. It wasn't the best title, but it resonated with me because it captured who I was. As a kid I would go to the temple, attend Hindu religious festivals, and watch Bollywood films, but I was also born in Britain and I was therefore British as well. I was a mixed bag of sweets, not one or the other, and at times this made me a little confused. There was always the pressure, though subtle at times, to conform and be the responsible eldest Asian son who looked after the family. But this was at loggerheads with the Western-inspired free spirit I was, who wanted to do what I wanted. In the Asian community I felt compelled to always try to give the right impression so as not to bring shame on my family. But I just couldn't carry on with all of that stuff any more. Why couldn't I embrace both cultures and just be BBA and Proud?

In writing the play I quickly hit a stumbling block. We had been asked to recruit actors from the university, but there just weren't any Asian drama students. And so began the long process of advertising for actors and auditioning. There were still hurdles ahead, most notably convincing a bunch of actors to work for free. I needed something to entice them. Most of them were out of work and wanted to fulfil their dream of acting.

And so I offered the actors an opportunity they simply couldn't refuse – an opportunity to take an extended version of the play to the Edinburgh Festival in the summer, as long as they agreed to offer their services for free for both the university production and the month-long run at the festival. They gladly accepted!

The Edinburgh Festival run took a toll on my health. I suddenly developed acid indigestion and have been taking tablets ever since. All the stress and pressure was causing bedlam with my stomach. After every performance came the scrutiny, further changes, and a demand on the actors to learn new lines. But as the festival drew to a close, the gamble was to pay off. The play ended up winning a Fringe First and with this accolade placed me in a strong position for Arts Council funding. The play wasn't particularly great. It was a bit clichéd, focusing on stereotypes. You know the stuff: parental pressure, repressed homosexual, the Asian who thinks he can pass for "white". The message of the play was a simple one: British-born Asians are often pretty "mixed up", a cultural cocktail. It might not have been well written – the reviews most certainly asserted that when it went on tour a year later – but nonetheless people flocked to see it. On reflection, it had been about timing. We were riding the crest of the wave. The TV series *Goodness Gracious Me* had first been televised in 1998 and had been a huge hit, making Asian culture cool. The tide had turned; the country was suddenly fascinated with us. For the first time I didn't need to act differently to be accepted, for the first time I felt OK in my brown skin. Suddenly my flighty ideas of "making it" quick weren't so flighty after all. When you have been to a school like Cavina, anything is possible.

With all the buzz around Asian culture, the play was spotted by a script editor who introduced me to a TV production company that quickly issued a contract to write a children's TV series called *My Life as a Popat* which followed the lives of a British-Indian family, through the eyes of their eldest son, Anand. Unlike with *BBA and Proud*, the TV production company had enough editors to help shape the writing, and thanks to them the two series would be aired on ITV and go on to win a BAFTA as well as being nominated for an International Emmy.

My life had become utterly crazy. I had become so driven that as soon as I had achieved one accolade I was after another. I was never relaxed enough to savour the joy of each achievement. The BAFTA was nice, but it didn't really mean anything. Going out to New York for the Emmy celebration was nice too, but my countenance would have probably been the same if I won it or not. I was nonchalant about such things. The only thing that really mattered was that I had finally had a taste of that little bit more. There was no one around me to rein me in. If I wanted to have a second chicken leg, I was going to have one! Marvin, the sheep, had reached the dizzy heights and found no joy when he got there. I was on the way up and I had no plans on getting sentimental like Marvin. How far could I go? One might ask, how long is a piece of string?

7

Prophecy Fulfilled

I had resigned myself to the fact that I probably wasn't ever going to have another relationship like the one I had had with Sarah. In all honesty, I wasn't looking to get into any serious relationship. But life had a way of doing its own thing. At my first teaching post I had met Maria. She was a very private, black science teacher, with a ready smile and wit to match. I used to see her regularly on the morning train and we would often walk to school together from the station.

I didn't read the signs, such as Maria linking my arm on the way to school or waiting for me in the pouring rain with an umbrella knowing full well I didn't have one. I thought she was just being friendly. This must have lasted for months until a friend of mine got drunk and spilled the beans. From then on I looked at Maria differently. I would observe her from afar, and I was intrigued about her nature. There was something in her spirit that was different. She had something that was absent in my life, though I couldn't put my finger on exactly what it was. She appeared to have an inner peace about her that was very attractive. Finally, I was decided. I walked into her science lab one afternoon after school and asked her out for a drink, only for her to surprise me by saying "no"! Somewhat bemused, I walked away, thinking that maybe my friend had made a mistake. And then I suddenly remembered how shy Maria was. Certain that this was the only reason she had declined, I confidently marched back into Maria's lab and proclaimed, "I think you meant to say 'yes'." My intuition was right. I have never seen a woman pack her bag to leave as quickly as she did then. Apparently, she had spent those few minutes in between me leaving and coming back to her lab cursing herself! Even though my bold move got the result I wanted, it was risky – I would not wholeheartedly recommend it, unless you enjoy being slapped.

Our first date that evening proved to be hard work. Around children, Maria beamed with confidence and was larger than life. The classroom has always been her theatre, where she both entertains and educates. However, around adults she could be incredibly shy and this was Maria's first proper date, so she was more shy than usual. I was about to close the door on any potential relationship with her, but before I could make up an excuse, Maria plucked up the courage to ask me if I wanted to go to the cinema the following week. I felt I had to say yes, but this following date turned out to be just as much hard work. Maria sat in silence throughout the film, and more periods of silence followed afterwards when we went to a nearby pub for a drink. I had pretty much decided that I was going to call it a day, but before I could concoct some story, Maria suggested going into London the following week. Wishing not to be rude I consented, and a week later we met up at Putney station, though this time she was totally unrecognizable. When I saw her I honestly thought it was someone else. Having bought a completely new outfit and gone to the hairdresser, Maria looked amazing. I spent the evening mesmerized by her new look and growing confidence.

In fact, I was so mesmerized that from that night, Maria and I pretty much moved in together. I don't think Maria envisaged it happening quite this way, but then I was an impulsive guy and thought she was a great girl. So why not just stay over, why not just move in? It wasn't like we had some meaningful conversation – should we, shouldn't we, maybe it is too early... That was not me. If you liked someone, you liked them. I decided not just for myself but for Maria as well, and quickly gave her a set of keys, telling her what was mine was hers. This had been my home, but now it would be *our* home.

Maria's family were from St Kitts and Nevis, and I was fascinated by her cultural background. I knew our relationship wouldn't go down well among some people, with racism still very much alive between the two communities. Some years later, I would listen with interest to a church pastor publicly confess how he had failed to share his faith with those from an Asian background because of the latent racism that existed within him. But Maria intrigued me, and I just knew we were meant to be together. It was like a force from somewhere had decided this was the way it was meant to be. In the years to come, Maria and I would often look in the mirror and say how strange we looked together – we are an odd couple! But something had brought us together and every time we were seen together we were making a statement about building bridges. When we went into a predominantly Asian area, we would often be met with stares. We still have to "suffer" meals in restaurants surrounded by people totally gobsmacked by our union. Today in modern Britain there are still very few mixed relationships between black and Asian people, and yet there are so many similarities in terms of our culture.

Sometime later, Maria shared with me how her mother, Georgina, had seen a vision before we had met in which God had shown her that her daughter would marry an Indian man and to welcome him into her home. At the time, Maria had liked a man from East Asia. But her mother was quick to clarify that the vision was of an Indian man. There were no mixed relationships in her family with Indians, so this would certainly be a first. I vividly recall the day I met Georgina, and how she welcomed me with open arms. Later she would confide in her daughter that I was the man she had seen in the vision.

Hearing about this supernatural premonition cemented in my mind that we were meant to be together. But it also left me with questions. Who was this God who spoke in visions, and what did our union mean? I later found out that Georgina was a Christian. Having turned my back on the Christian God, I suddenly found myself being connected to a Christian family. But any apprehension I might have had was diffused by Georgina's kindness. She never once shared her faith with me, and to be honest, that suited me fine. As for Maria, she had been brought up in the black Pentecostal church but her faith had become dormant not long after her beloved grandfather had died. Maria's real dad had left when she was younger, and so she had called her grandfather her dad. She was devastated when he passed away, and with that her connection with the church had fizzled out.

I often remarked to Maria that there was something different about her mother. I couldn't comprehend her joy. It wasn't like any other joy I had seen. Life had not been easy for her with cancer, an abusive relationship, and being a single mum to three, but there was no bitterness or rage. Instead there appeared to be a grateful spirit for all she had, a genuine contentment about her council flat and work in a nearby shop. Whenever I asked her deep questions, her answers would be loaded with wisdom and authority. Where did these answers come from? I could see traces of Georgina in Maria, and together they pointed to a different world, a better world. They never spoke about what they did in unseen ways for others, but I watched with curiosity as I caught glimpses of their compassion and generosity to people they hardly knew.

Georgina was a private person and seldom spoke about her own life. Yet over time I found out about her battle with cancer and how despite her illness she never felt alone. She still regularly visited the hospital for checks and she spoke about how the chair next to her in the waiting room would always be empty – nobody would sit there, as if it was reserved for someone unseen who was attending with Georgina. When Maria had been only ten years old, her mother had ended up in hospital in critical condition. The doctor had said that they had lost her only for her to come back. What had happened in those moments when she was "gone"? What did she see? She must have seen something that had impacted her life. Girdhardas had come to visit me to tell me something after he had sadly passed away. Yes, it was to look after his wife, but it seemed more cryptic than just keeping an eye on her daily welfare. In Georgina I met someone who had come back from death, and though she said very little I began to realize that she too had some kind of message for me. But what did it all mean?

When I used to go with Maria to visit Georgina, I would relish the opportunity to take time out from the frantic life I had made for myself. Georgina offered yet another perspective to add to those expressed by others

I had met along the journey of life, yet my desire to succeed would always get the better of me. I wanted it all and I wanted it quickly – and now that meant enlisting the help of Maria. She had a natural ability to write, and a wicked sense of humour. I would one day be receiving the praise, but in reality it was Maria who would be doing all the hard work, penning much of the *BBA and Proud* play and the TV series *My Life as a Popat*. It was a great partnership – Maria hated the limelight, but was happy to work harder than most behind the scenes; I was her frontman! I had a knack of surrounding myself with people who were far better than me in the areas I was lacking. My job was simply to inspire people into participation.

Maria calls this "high-class delegation".

8

The Cash Convertor

Writing and directing had been OK. It had brought me recognition and a nice award for the mantelpiece. But in truth, with all the entertainment industry glitz and excitement, I was still left wanting. I could have carried on, and I am sure I could have churned out another play or possibly even a film if I got lucky, but the obvious drawback was time. This would all take *time* and I wanted money *now* so I began to turn my interest to business. The idea of starting my own business had been spinning around in my mind since my childhood days in Kenya. But what business would I do? I had considered a number of ideas, from setting up a beauty salon for the metrosexual man to selling fun one-day packages to train your hubby to become a domesticated god. And then one day it just happened.

I don't recall ever making a conscious decision to get into the property game. It was simply something I drifted into, swept along by the tide of house price growth and the media's obsessive coverage of the upturn in the economy. It was the mid-nineties, and having come out of a difficult economic period, dinner table conversation was once again turning to how much the family home could appreciate in value. Clearly, new opportunities were on the horizon as the housing market entered a period of growth. Just how high could house prices go in this latest cycle? If prices continued to increase, just maybe the country could start dreaming again. Dreaming of selling a three-bed semi for a luxury villa in sunny Spain. Dreaming of getting out of the London rat race for a more sedate life in the pretty English countryside. Indeed, for a country of homeowners, the property pie was once again beginning to look rather enticing, and throughout the country people were gathering like vultures to eagerly eye up a chunky slice.

The potential looked too good to be true. Those in previous years who had made a bundle through property price growth were free of the system of having to work just to pay bills, bills, and more bills. And as far as I was concerned, one thing you really couldn't put a price on was freedom. I had barely begun my working life, and yet the importance of gaining freedom was at the top of my list of priorities. Certainly, if "freedom" was being offered for sale at an auction, I would most definitely be lining up a series of hefty bids. I was sold on the kind of life that bricks and mortar had to offer, and thus began my foray into the world of property wheeling and dealing.

I had already saved up part of my first deposit during my year out after university. On completing my degree,

I had toyed with the idea of managing an indie band. That didn't work out, and so Sarah and I had applied for teacher training the following year, leaving me with six months to earn some money. The job centre conjured up a two-week job serving coffee to customers during the launch of a new furniture store. This wasn't ideal, especially while other graduates were ahead of the game in some graduate scheme within a top firm. I had to get my act together and put my brain to use. And so, while serving coffee I began to learn about the furniture we were selling. It was nice stuff, particularly the company's own range of handmade sofas, made to measure, fully sprung with a lifetime guarantee. Twenty years later, my mother still sits on one of these handmade settees.

What I began to realize as I served the coffee to prospective buyers was that this really wasn't a hard sell. You could buy the sofa on finance with interest-free credit, so it was just a matter of making them comfortable with the product so that they were tempted enough to part with a deposit. By the end of the month I had passed so many leads to my work colleagues that the store manager had taken notice, and after a word with the regional manager I was offered a permanent job. And thus began my journey into the world of sales.

Within months my arrogance levels were hitting the roof as I became the top salesperson in the shop, and one of the top salespeople across the thirty furniture stores. Before I had been a coffee boy, but now I had deservedly earned my place on the company elite sales force and there was no stopping me. Boy, was I thankful to those weeks of serving coffee; that was where I had learnt my craft. To be perfectly honest, the art was to do anything but "sell". I would spend all my time chatting to customers about anything and everything but the furniture, and that consistently seemed to do the trick. Customers hate pushy salespeople following them around the shop floor and so I would leave them well alone. After all, if they were interested in the product they would eventually come and ask for assistance. Each salesperson could write their personal version of the art of selling. My strategy was plain and simple. Relax. Do not pressure-sell. Don't talk about the product until pushed to do so. They'll love you for it, and as a sweet thank you, they'll even buy the product you wanted to sell them in the first place! Oh, and don't forget the coffee. Always serve them coffee. And real coffee at that; Douwe Egberts coffee. Smells good, tastes good; well worth the effort of making when they are signing on the dotted line half an hour later.

I loved the psychology of it all. It really wasn't rocket science. I just couldn't get those guys who kept on using "sales patter" that consistently failed to work. If only they could be still for a moment and take the time to analyse the situation.

I was ecstatic when I was chosen to be part of a small select group to sell furniture at the annual Ideal Home Show. What young lad would refuse the opportunity to rake in the kind of money this experience had to offer? What's more, the show would provide the perfect battleground to prove just how good I really was. The stakes were high. In three weeks one could potentially earn the equivalent of six months' salary. As expected, the sales team were cut-throat and would not think twice about stealing your customers from under your nose. Over the three weeks I made £6,000 in commission – a nice tidy sum to help me get on the property ladder.

The rest of the deposit would come from my most generous parents. They were far from wealthy but despite this, they were still eager to dig deep into their savings to help me out. That's Asian parents for you! Sometimes they can be a tad interfering but one thing's for sure, you are hard pushed to find an Asian family who won't go that extra mile for their children. My parents had made one wrong decision that had had a domino effect on the rest of their lives. I was hell-bent on not making the same mistake. I saw property as the way forward. I was going to be successful, financially secure, and self-reliant. And so with the help of my parents, combined with the money I had earned at the Ideal Home Show, I finally found myself on the property ladder and even had a little left over to begin doing it up.

My first property was a little Victorian terrace in Wandsworth. Positioned next to a bustling one-way system and a noisy railway line, the property was by no means easy on the ears. Furthermore, as it backed on to a council depot, it was unsightly to say the least. But as far as I was concerned it had a lot going for it. For starters, it had bags of space. For £110,000 I had got a small four-bedroom house for the same price as a one-bed flat in East Putney. People probably thought I was crazy for purchasing a home that had failed to sell for several months, but I could see something in the property that others had failed to consider. It was a stone's throw from East Putney; literally a road away to be exact. I was also certain that eventually people would be priced-out of the desirable roads and forced to reconsider this street. It was a major risk, but one I relished with enthusiasm. The gamble paid off and within two years, "yuppies" started moving into the area, and property developers began chopping up the houses into flats. After selling my first home two and a half years later for more than double the price I had originally paid for it, I had most certainly caught the property bug.

And the marriage bug! Feeling financially secure I could now turn my attention to marrying Maria. Bless her, she had waited long enough for me to ask her, but the timing had never felt quite right. At the end of the day it all boiled down to being able to provide sufficiently financially in order to feel free to pop the question. Maria went on about "love", and of course love was important, but getting married in the real world meant being able to provide a home and an income for the family. We got engaged in the Brecon Beacons in a delightful cottage in the picturesque countryside. When I finally asked Maria, she initially said "no"! It was déjà vu. Remember, Maria had said "no" when I asked her out! Thankfully, after she had run around for a while, she settled down and then blurted out with excitement and no "help" from me – "I mean yes, yes!"

And so things were settled. We were to get married at a nearby hotel a year later. It would be the hottest day of the year, and prove to be a great merging of two cultures. I was astounded by the way in which Maria's family came along for a run-through of the Hindu ceremony I had opted for. Were they not Christians? Maria had agreed with the idea, and so if she was OK with it maybe they were too. In any event, I never once got the impression that they weren't. I was hugely impacted by their willingness to embrace my culture and respect my Hindu faith. This really was an incredibly special family I had been connected to.

I was blessed to have Maria as a part of my life, but in having got married I instantly felt the responsibility land on my shoulders to ensure that I provided well for my family. My parents had separated years prior due to the issue of finances. I was absolutely certain I was not going to make the mistakes they had made. I was already my own boss and therefore in charge of my destiny. As long as I had a discerning eye and did my research well, property would bring me the success I craved. I was doing what any good husband would do. Providing for your wife was a given, and I definitely wasn't going to let Maria down!

9

All Smoke and Mirrors

aving opted to cash in, we briefly moved into a rented property. However, the lure of buying another property was beginning to preoccupy me. I wasn't slow to catch on to a trend and I needed little persuasion. As a youngster I was addicted to the sensation of smoking in the cool morning breeze with a cup of coffee. And now property was to be the drug that satisfied my cravings. The calculations made perfect sense. Why earn interest on £10,000 in a bank account, when you can invest £10,000 in a property and effectively earn interest on the whole value of the property as it appreciates in value? It all made logical sense, and thus began my assault into the world of property trading.

After making a quick turn on a few apartments I had purchased, my eye suddenly caught the attention of buying off-plan. Now, this was a wholly different ball game! Whereas, in my early investments I had to go through the palaver of renting and maintaining the properties, buying off-plan offered a far more attractive proposition, for here was the possibility of becoming an armchair investor. What could be better than reaping the rewards without having to exhaust myself putting in the hours? I'd buy the property while it was still a plan on the architect's drawing board and then, thanks to ever-rising property prices, sell it on, perhaps before it had even been built, for a profit. All that was required of me was to put a deposit down, sit back, and watch the property appreciate in value. While close acquaintances of mine were running around trying to keep up with maintaining their buy-to-let portfolio, I was relaxing in cafés drinking cappuccinos and ogling *The Sun*. The strategy was simple. If I failed to move the property on before it was built, I could either sell it when ready, or failing that, let it out, which had the added advantage of it having few maintenance issues because it was a new build. I was completely hooked on the concept, and from here onwards all my property transactions were in the off-plan residential market.

And the rest is history! Within months I had made a name for myself as someone to go and speak to regarding buying off-plan properties, and before I knew it I had a queue of people wanting to buy apartments from me. Talk about fast-tracking! I set up a company with my mother in 2003 and overnight we became known as the wheeling and dealing middlemen trading in the buying and selling of city-centre new-build apartments. The process was simple. My property company would cut deals with high-profile developers. In some instances we would reserve whole blocks of apartments at a time before flipping on the contracts to investors before a spade was put in the ground. Our profit margin was the difference between the purchase price and selling price, which I would receive on completion of the development. Rocket science? No way! Truly, there was no real art to this kind of property trading. Find a developer, negotiate a discount, put a deposit down, and sell on the apartment contract at a higher price. I had found a model that worked for all parties. The developer got their sale, the investor got the property they were after, and I made a tidy sum as the conduit between them.

Talk about an exponential rise. One minute I was buying a few apartments around the Hertfordshire area and the next selling hundreds of apartments in new-build schemes across the country. We were an overnight sensation! We were actually doing what many could only hope to do in their wildest dreams. I enjoyed the admiration that came my way. But what do you expect when one minute you're a nobody in the business world and the next you're the latest mover and shaker on the scene? Yet with a bit of maturity and reflection, which has been a very long time coming, I am able to give credit where credit is due. I may have been good on the front line, but behind the scenes it was actually my mother who was holding the fort.

Unquestionably, I couldn't have managed without my mother, and in her I certainly found the perfect business partner. Incredibly reliable and with a close eye for detail, she would prove to be the rock upon which the company would grow and flourish. Having experienced her fair share of setbacks in life, here was a fantastic opportunity for my mother to put things right and she relished the challenge. Kenya had been a complete waste and the ensuing years in England had been particularly difficult, but as far as she was concerned both grit and determination would finally win the day. The school of hard knocks had taught her a lesson or two about never giving up. Harriet Beecher Stowe's famous words that we should never give up, for that is just the time and place when the tide would turn spring to mind when I think of my mother. In Kenya she had baked cakes to make ends meet. Back in England in her forties she had gone back to college in the evenings to study A-level accounts and subsequently other accountancy qualifications so that she could carve out a future career. Perseverance was her forte. She was like a tractor with an endless fuel supply. She just kept on ploughing ahead.

However, the more apartments we sold and the more renowned we became, the greater the challenge we faced to keep a lid on the true reality behind the scenes. As most of the schemes had a two- to three-year build programme, I would have to wait a while before I could count my millions. And what's more, property developers were notorious for overrunning the build course. A two-year build programme could quite easily turn into a four-year build programme. So what was the problem? Let me explain. We were perceived to be the flash people with the cash. Yet the reality was far removed from these perceptions. I may have been running a multi-million pound business, but I was simply rich on paper. It was like I had signed up to buy a Ferrari but I wasn't allowed to drive it yet. As far as my customers were concerned, they probably thought I was coughing up money and living in a big house in the country. Indeed, one day when the developments would come round to completion I may just be driving that Ferrari and living in that big house in Hampstead Heath but for the time being I would have to settle for my Honda Jazz and my neat and tidy semi in middle-class suburbia. Now, don't get me wrong, I love Japanese cars and there certainly isn't anything wrong with a car that has probably won every award under the sun. But to only be able to afford to drive one of those when you're running a large-scale operation like the one we were running was causing me a headache. My investors were buying into the dream that they could be "rich" like me as long as they bought our apartments. Shatter the image and you shatter the dream. And shattering the dream would mean no sale!

Clearly, there was no way I could afford the reality of my situation to become public knowledge. Just how long could I continue to hide this secret, a secret that I couldn't possibly afford to get out if I was going to fulfil my dream of becoming "filthy rich"? How long could I continue to park my car two streets away so that I avoided being spotted by a potential investor? How long could I hold meetings in cafés as my office was nothing more than my 9ft study in my semi-detached house?

The truth of the situation was that the cash simply hadn't filtered through and every day I felt like I was living a double life. I had no intention of having things pan out this way, but the business simply grew too quickly. And so I was forced into using an agency to take my calls and work out of a PO box address. You are probably thinking that if I was doing these multi-million pound deals I must have had a big pot of cash to work out of. However, the reality was quite the contrary. The school of life had given me a Masters in creative accounting. Let me elaborate. From the small pot of money I had, I was able to fund the reservation of apartments. Typically, I would then be given eight weeks to exchange contracts and find exchange monies of approximately 5 to 10 per cent of the purchase price of the properties. I reckoned that if I could find enough buyers to purchase the apartments, on the day I exchanged contracts with the developer, my buyers could exchange contracts with me, thereby enabling me to use my buyers' exchange deposits to fund my exchange deposit. Each deal we did was therefore a race against time to find sufficient buyers for the deal to work, and with no advertising budget, all I could do was get down and network.

Yes, I admit, I was a high risk-taker. There wasn't a challenge I would say "no" to. And so when I got the chance to do a deal of purchasing 220 apartments in Leeds, I jumped at the opportunity. The value of the building was over £30 million, and as the lawyers set to work, I got cracking on finding buyers that would fund the £1.5 million I needed on exchange of contracts. Over a two-month period I spent day and night visiting one investor after another. OK, so some previous buyers helped me to find investors in exchange for commission, but that went only so far in aiding me to get the £1.5 million I needed. I don't quite know what had got into me. I was like a man possessed, not so much by the prospect of making a million here or there on completion of the apartments, but on the adrenalin rush of making the impossible a possibility. It was all about being creative and thinking laterally. Yes, a part of me wanted to be rich, but the artistry used in *becoming* that rich guy was also important to me.

In truth, it was all smoke and mirrors. There was no big buyer as such. I was conducting my empire from the smallest room in my semi-detached house and using the funds my buyers paid me on exchange of contracts. I could have opted for a more risk averse business model like many of the property clubs who acted as agents making a tidy sum through earning commission from the developer plus a finders' fee from the buyer. A nice little earner, but oh, so terribly boring! This is where I wanted to go against the grain. I wasn't interested in selling something I didn't truly believe in. *Would I buy it myself?* The reality was there were loads of property clubs selling properties they wouldn't have touched with a barge pole. That is where my company differed. We would ourselves exchange on the contracts. If it all went belly-up we would be accountable. The risks were higher but the profit margins were also greater. Some years before, I had also sold my mother a three-piece suite because I believed in the furniture we were selling. Just because I had moved on in life didn't mean I was prepared to compromise on that. I would only sell what I was prepared to buy myself.

It truly baffled me how the developers got away with selling entire blocks of apartments to me. It had all come about with a bit of luck. Brought up to believe that first impressions count, I recall paying a visit to a large estate agent one day and dropping in a very nice bottle of champagne for the person in charge of residential sales. As expected, I made the right impression, and immediately got a call, but what I hadn't predicted was the sudden offers that came my way to transact on millions of pounds-worth of new-build contracts. Crazy as it may sound, not only did the developers transact with me, but the majority of them did so without their bankers doing any detailed checks on my company. OK, so I may have talked a good talk, but if the developers and their banks had dug deeper they would have certainly noticed that I was all fur coat and no knickers. However, looking back on it I don't view them to be at fault. The person I was would have made sure they had no choice but to sell to me. It was all so crazy, yet exciting at the same time.

10

Spin Doctor

═══════════

Margaret Thatcher invented it, Tony Blair made it an art form, and I thought I could use it as well. I didn't have a large sales team and there was no way I could afford to complete on all of these transactions. But then again, what could possibly go wrong when you're in bed with a public relations agency?

Public relations (PR) was my latest idea. I wanted to see just how far I could take this business model, and so I had hired a PR agency to run a press release on my acquisition of the 220 apartments I had bought in Leeds. This could transport me into a whole new arena. Just maybe, one day I could be mixing with the big boys. This could be the break that could catapult me from being just rich into *The Sunday Times* Rich List.

I vividly recall the day I got a phone call stating that a journalist loved the tale. It was to be a rags to riches story of how a humble teacher became a property tycoon buying up blocks of apartments across the north of England. As you can imagine, I was absolutely ecstatic.

The photo-shoot took place in the show apartment of the £1 million marketing suite of the swanky development of apartments I had invested in. I felt like royalty as I sat down on the enormous circular chair. Set upon a shiny silvery base, this majestic chair, made of ocean blue and cream leather, was indeed an ostentatious piece of furniture – just what was required to catch the eye of the impending readers. What better location could there be than this? Positioned next to a dock, this was Leeds' newest and most exciting leisure and shopping complex. On completion, this new development scheme would be one of the largest mixed-use developments outside of London, and would include over 1,000 city-centre apartments, chic designer shops, quality restaurants, and a casino, all set around the atmospheric dock. One day, you would be able to stroll out of your luxurious apartment and straight into a full-height glazed space selling the latest in cutting-edge trends or serving contemporary cuisine from around the world.

I tried to act cool as the photographers swanned around me but underneath, I was bubbling with excitement. I felt like the Don. And better still, all eyes were on me, especially the ladies'. One of the perks of buying new apartments was that you could always guarantee pretty women in short skirts to be employed to sell on the bricks and mortar. I was finally receiving the fruits of my labour. As I sat on my deserved throne, I truly felt invincible. Nothing could touch me. Nothing could stop me from becoming filthy rich!

Recently, I had come to appreciate that everything has a life span. I wasn't getting any younger. At present I was relatively easy on the eye, but there would be a time when I would lose all the hair on my head and look anything but trendy. I knew I had to milk it while I could, and sending out the press release was part of that decision. And that was the very reason why I justified spending money on fine suits, like the one that was getting attention at this photo-shoot.

I could have gone to Savile Row, but instead I had opted for a smallish London tailor called Mr Eddie. This was a low-key father and son operation. Just how I liked it: old school, traditional, and making classy suits. No credit cards, but just cash and cheques taken. Here you could get a suit for £600 and look a cut above the rest, and what's more you had the added bonus of being able to share a pleasant little story about the tailor you got it from. A nice talking point. People love stories. My mother thought I was being extravagant. Well, I begged to differ. If only my mother could hear the comments I was getting. For me it all made logical sense. If I was going to successfully sell apartments, I needed to first sell the dream that you too could wear a suit just like me if you signed on the dotted line. And the same principle applied to the shoes I was wearing. Prior to going to university, I had bought an expensive pair of

Oxford toe caps while working at Gordon Scott's. My mother may have thought I was extravagant, but it was through extravagance that I had finally come to roost.

Generally speaking, very little fazes me. However, nothing had prepared me for the subsequent article in *The Daily Telegraph* about my property company. I was expecting a small article and definitely not the entire front and most of the second page of the property section. The reality only started to sink in as my mobile phone began ringing with calls from new customers via the telephone agency that acted as a virtual secretary for my business. You can imagine the amazement when people were answered by "yours truly" – we were such a small outfit we didn't even have a secretary. Well, what could I do but take the calls and make some comment like "I am a hands-on kind of boss"? The impact of the article was beyond my wildest imagination. We were to sell hundreds and hundreds of apartments on the back of it. The gamble had indeed paid off.

Now that success and money had become my god, I turned to PR in a big way. Sad as it may sound, PR was to become my closest friend and ally. Who needs a close set of friends when you can run an article in a newspaper and get all the attention you could possibly desire? PR and I were one happy couple. Although my company had been growing nicely, it was PR that would form the catalyst to my rise and fame. There only so many people I could physically meet and sell apartments to, and PR provided me with access to a new group of people who wanted a slice of the action. It was PR that would give me access to all those investors who had bought into the dream of buying an investment property early on in the build programme so that they could cash in on completion when the property had risen in value. Pensions had failed to deliver, as had the stock market. But with property, you could never go wrong. An Englishman's home is his castle. As far as I was concerned, the same principle applied to one's buy-to-let investment portfolio. They were all castles. The question was, who could own the most and be the biggest king of them all?

In time I reread the newspaper article in *The Daily Telegraph* and noticed just how vague I had been about how I was running my property ship. That would have to remain my little secret. So what next? Well, onwards and upwards. Why stop? The economy was thriving, land was in short supply, and with a growing population, house prices were guaranteed to keep on rising. Indeed, as long as the government kept on ranting and raving about the need for 3 million new homes by 2020, I had a most lucrative career ahead of me. It was simply a matter of supply and demand, and with demand fearlessly outstripping supply, the future was good – the future was Manoj!

Article in *The Daily Telegraph*

A Vision of the North

By Angela Pertusini
Published: 10 September 2005

Manoj Raithatha began his road to riches in an unsalubrious street in Wandsworth.

Five years ago, Manoj Raithatha was a struggling teacher-cum-playwright in south London. Today, he's making a fortune, wheeling and dealing in flats in the North. How does he do it? Angela Pertusini meets him in Leeds.

Manoj Raithatha makes it all sound so reasonable. Why wouldn't you buy 209 apartments in a yet-to-be-built block in Leeds? Why not spend £35 million on one big day out? He shrugs, he smiles, he makes perfect sense. I begin to feel a bit sheepish that I haven't thought of doing it myself.

Although his purchase at Crosby Homes, Clarence Dock, in Leeds, is thought to be the biggest single deal in the North this year, such shopping sprees, even on this epic scale, are becoming increasingly commonplace for Manoj.

As well as this most recent "230, no 220, um 200 or something in that region", he casually mentions that he has also just bought 120 in the La Salle block next door and negotiated with Knight Frank for a further 103 round the corner in Cartier House.

On top of which he has 10 or 11 in a block (whose name no one can remember), on the opposite bank of the Aire, which he bought about 18 months ago.

And, as well as his big-spending in Leeds, he has been emptying the developers' shelves in Liverpool, Bradford, Hull and Sheffield, where he has bought a block of 140 flats near the city centre. "Sheffield is an interesting place," he says. "The money being pumped into that city and Hull is phenomenal." Manoj has high hopes for Hull.

Five years ago, Manoj didn't own any property at all. He had been teaching English and drama in a school in Brixton, south London, and was studying for an MA that he hoped would act as a launchpad for his real passion, writing.

In 2000, while completing his degree, he wrote a play, BBA and Proud, in which he managed to persuade some of his co-students to perform.

"The BBA stands for British-born Asian. I thought it was a great title at the time, but, yeah, now I'm a bit embarrassed," he says. They took the play to the Edinburgh Festival where, ta-raaa, it scooped an Edinburgh Fringe First prize and a professional theatre company then offered Manoj a national tour.

He should have been felt flushed [sic] with success, but the life of a struggling artist didn't really appeal. "It just doesn't pay that well, I realised. So I had to think of some way of making extra money."

Admitting to being a bit of a wheeler and dealer by nature, Manoj plumped for property speculation. He owned a small house in the then scabby bit of Wandsworth, south-west London – bought, he confesses, because he couldn't afford neighbouring Putney – and, renting out two rooms to friends to cover the mortgage, he watched the value double in a couple of years.

This was an easy way to make money, he decided. Being the owner of just one puny house myself, it is this next stage, the bit where he goes from modest owner-occupier to 450 flats in one city alone, that interests me most.

I wait impatiently, pen poised greedily, but Manoj is frustratingly vague. He shrugs, he smiles. I smile encouragingly back but I need detail, I need tips; damn it, I need him to write me a 10-step How to Become a Property Tycoon plan. But Manoj is hard to pin down.

What I do pick up is that he didn't follow the well-worn route – the sun-bleached skeletons of would-be property developers litter its kerb – of finding a shabby flat and doing it up à la Property Ladder. Immaculate in his zippy suit, embroidered shirt and Beckham-style diamond earstuds, Manoj does not look the type of person who would be at one with a wallpaper-scraper.

No, he started by using proceeds from the Wandsworth house sale to buy several flats at once in Harrow (at least he thinks it was Harrow, it might have been his home town of Watford, he concedes).

How? They were virtual flats – bought off-plan and requiring an outlay of only 10 per cent of their price to "buy" them, the rest not due until completion, which could be several months, even a year or more away. All he had to do was keep his nerve and, as prices soared – up by 21 per cent in London from 2001–2002 – so did his investments.

Having exchanged contracts, the builders were tied to selling Manoj the properties at the original prices but – and here's the first clever bit – Manoj could raise further money himself by either remortgaging at the new, higher value or selling the flats on before completing upon them.

It was a brilliant business idea and one that the rest of us Jeremiahs, convinced that the end of the boom was nigh, were unable to replicate.

As news of the canny deal-making spread, members of his Ugandan-Asian family started to ask him to invest money on their behalf; then their friends. "Over one weekend we ended up buying 30 flats," says Manoj cheerfully. Through his company, Summertime Properties, he now has a client base of about 800 people, all interested in following his lead.

With that extra money comes extra muscle. By buying a tranche of flats from one developer, he was able to negotiate on price.

"You can usually get 10–15 per cent off if you're volume buying but, if you are buying a whole block, you might get 20 per cent." He keeps a few of the flats for himself and the rest he sells back to his investors – they pay more than he paid for the flats but less than the developer's list price.

So, the second clever bit is that not only does he get his hands on a hopefully appreciating asset but, should the worst happen, he might still have a property that … is worth more in a recession than the price he paid for it.

Not that Manoj feels a recession is a likely outcome for Leeds. Sitting in Crosby Homes' swanky marketing suite, he is king of practically all he surveys, from the already-built blocks that surround us to the barely-off-the-architect's board schemes he has so heavily backed just recently.

"I came across Leeds completely by accident at a property show," he says with disarming honesty. "There was a buzz about it so I visited and I was blown away. It's pretty small but it's got fantastic facilities."

Ask him if the city might not be a little overstocked with this sort of waterside, luxury apartment development and he pooh-poohs the idea. "The main reason we've invested here is the economy. The finance sector is very strong – 17 out of 20 of the top legal practices in the country have offices here, and there's the Bank of England. As long as that's expanding, it's fine."

OK, he seems convincing on Leeds, but what about rather less buzzy Bradford and Hull, which recently came first in Channel 4's Worst Places in Britain survey?

"I'm really interested in regeneration," he says. "Crosby Homes has done some wonderful work here in Leeds, but we've worked with Urban Splash, which goes into an area and regenerates it, and that's something I'm keen on. We've also bought from Newmason Properties, which is passionate about improving an area. It isn't just about how much money they can rake in."

For someone who is buying property purely as an investment, whose company ethos is based on making profits from canny purchases, money is an issue for Manoj. When I ask him if he has ever had his fingers burnt, he looks shocked. "No. Never," he says firmly. Ask him who recces out the areas he decides to buy in and he takes full responsibility.

Summertime Properties may be essentially a property club (although, unlike many others, clients do not have to pay a joining or a subscription fee and Manoj buys the properties he offers, rather than simply reserves them), but it is unusual in that one person seems to be in charge of all the major decisions and takes control of the negotiations: "I would never leave that to someone else," he says aghast.

Nevertheless, despite many of us considering such a workload a full-time job, with his wife Maria, he still managed to write a series, *My Life as a Popat*, which was nominated for a Royal Television Society award last year.

I have a last stab at working out his formula and making my millions – which, say, I could combine with life as a successful award-winning novelist. How easy has it been for him? Is it something, and here I blush modestly, that anyone could do? He shrugs, he smiles. "I've been really lucky. I suppose you just have to be a bit of risk-taker."

11

Cracks in the Pavement

W hen you have money, people fall into two groups – people who want to be *near* you and jealous people who want to *be* you. Maria was odd. She failed to fit into either camp. I thrived on the attention of others. Yet beneath the surface all was not well. Small cracks were becoming great chasms in me and with my relationships with my wife and friends. Even if I had wanted to stop I wouldn't have known how to. I had become an addict – addicted to making money, addicted to being successful, addicted to showing the world how good I was. I had got on the treadmill and rather than slowing occasionally for some respite, I found myself stepping up another gear. The treadmill was moving at a reckless pace and I could barely keep up. But I just couldn't slow it down. London was a buzz of activity and I needed to be at the centre of it all. The thought of stopping was easily rebuked. This was my life. This was all I knew. As long as I carried on, I had a chance of being even richer and therefore a chance of gaining even greater happiness. And yet with each step, I seemed to become less and less content with life. I was on a road to self-destruction but the momentum was too great to stop.

In itself, the experience of having money meant little to me. Now, I wanted money and all the trappings that came with it. But the thought of having made my millions through a lottery ticket filled me with utter dread. Where was the satisfaction in being given money when you could experience the joy of earning it? Don't get me wrong, we can all do with a helping hand. My parents had most certainly given me a good start with a decent education and a generous contribution towards the deposit I needed for my first home. But that was where I drew the line. The world is full of people who want handouts and that was a world I wanted to be as far removed from as possible. I wanted meaning and purpose in life, and it was in rising to the challenge of making money that I was convinced I would find it.

The last year, 2007, had been particularly insane. The risks were getting greater and greater. I was buying apartments in areas I hadn't even visited on the basis of being able to sell them before I'd need to. The thing is, I didn't want to miss out and I definitely did not want someone to profit where I could have done. The potential was there to make money and I'd be crazy to let that opportunity pass me by. Property prices were still rising rapidly and my business had just reported a big surge in profits.

Towards the end of 2007 I found myself acquiring my dream home located in a private gated estate. I recall standing in the garden one day, looking at the house and feeling that I had truly made it. All those years of hard work and determination had finally paid off. There was the potential to triple the size of the existing house into a majestic seven-bed seven-bath house with all the gadgets to go with it – within just ten minutes of seeing it, I was sold. I offered the asking price, deciding to purchase the property as a surprise gift for my wife. But my wife wasn't after the big extravagant displays. She would have been happy with an interesting book or an hour with me at a local café. But I was lost in an increasingly unreal world and convinced that this, rather than emotional trust, was what would delight her. After all, it was our anniversary, and how better to profess my love than buying a house in a private estate? I was sure she would like it; what was there not to like? What woman wouldn't want a gift like this? We were going up in the world and she would be the envy of others!

Surely now you would think that there would be a little peace and time to rest. But the feeling didn't last and within weeks I had picked up another house in the estate with new dreams of buying several more when the cash allowed, dreaming that having quantity could eventually give me power to determine house prices and one day make a packet. My head was full of all this kind of stuff. That is how I thought, that is how I operated. Bizarre to some, but normal to me.

It is an understatement to say I had well and truly fallen for making money, and the impact of this could be seen in my family life. Yes, I took the odd holiday, but even during these times away my mind was not with my family. I was so caught up in succeeding that I forgot to spend time with them. I could buy my kids a great education and grand holidays, but what they really wanted was quality time. They wanted my undivided attention. Some years later, I recall being on holiday and sitting down with my children to watch a DVD when they said that this was the best day of their holiday. How my lack of being there for them in the past resonated that day.

As for my wife, Maria, she bore the brunt of my addiction. We were chalk and cheese. She liked visiting historical sites, reading deep, meaningful prose, and watching documentaries and highbrow programmes, whereas I liked *The Sun*, football, and money. She was content with a small house whereas I wanted it large. She was happy shopping in discount stores whereas I was opting for the designers. You couldn't have put us together. The money never got to her head. We could have been living in a box and she would have been just as happy. I was seldom at home in the evenings, but still Maria never walked out on me. We were spending less and less time together, and when we did I was bringing my ruthless business streak into the home. And on top of this, I began to cultivate a terrible temper to match.

I asked Maria to write a candid version of this period from her point of view. Sometimes, it can be painful to look at yourself in the past and through the eyes of others. I wish I had had this hindsight ten years ago.

Maria's story

I try not to think about this time. It is too light to say this was a difficult period. I felt each day I was losing my husband; the kind-hearted guy in a cardigan; the fun-loving man who promised to always cherish me. I often wondered where he was late at night but any hint that he was being unfaithful was faced with a barrage of indignation, denials, and cold shoulders. I felt I was literally left holding the baby while Manoj enjoyed the high life. I became my own worst enemy, retreating into my own private world, not communicating my hurt. Manoj was the successful businessman everyone wanted to be near, so who would listen? I had become more isolated from my friends and family, and spent many a lonely time lamenting about my marriage. I felt powerless to stop the growing chasm between us. Manoj was well-loved by all so I convinced myself that voicing my concerns would have been quickly shot down. These thoughts were upheld by countless people telling me how lucky I was to have a successful businessman for a husband. They judged how good a marriage was by the big house or the flash car. Life for them was broken down into a collection of essential status symbols that had to be fought for like a demented form of Monopoly. They were totally unaware that these material objects failed to give me happiness or peace. I was the odd one that was not enjoying Manoj's rise.

He had become very flash with the cash with a number of friends in high places. I did not go to the fancy restaurants, and after a while, he did not ask me. I was not posh, just pure council. I felt he was embarrassed to be seen with me which was confirmed when I overheard a hanger-on expressing her amazement that he could be with a woman like me.

Major decisions were no longer made together. Manoj bought a family home in a sought-after area without my knowledge. To cap this I returned to our home at the time to find our possessions in a removal van. Manoj had decided we were moving to this new property that day. No discussion. No argument. This behaviour was met with laughter and slaps on the back from his friends. Everyone accepted his compulsive, impulsive behaviour in a positive manner. How could I answer against the majority?

Money is good – you need it to get by and to help others with less. However, it can also change people and families for the worse overnight. I felt like a stranger in my own home.

Money had various facets, I knew, but I didn't really take the time to consider its darker side. It had its purposes and that was enough for me. But the love of it was highly explosive. My life had started like a completed jigsaw puzzle, with all the pieces intact and perfectly joined together. I had been happy with the simple things, content with living in our little terrace in Watford, watching *Top of the Pops*, and knocking my football against the wall of our house. Even the caravan holidays, to be perfectly honest, were great times away. I was happy and I didn't really desire for anything – other than an extra chicken leg! But once that seed of having more had been sown, innocence had quickly been replaced with greed. Instead of valuing people, it became about building empires and new kingdoms. And then, one by one, the pieces of the puzzle had started to come apart. I had gone too far; I was disintegrating.

I was aware that the cracks were there, but refused to address them because to do so would have revealed that I was the problem, and this was not a truth I was ready to accept. After all, wasn't I doing what any good husband would do by providing a luxurious lifestyle for my wife and children? What more could they ask for as they enjoyed this beautiful private island in Mauritius? OK, so I spent a lot of my time checking and responding to my emails, but what did they expect? There was too much money involved to switch off. The company was already turning over millions and the best was yet to come, with a pipeline of over 800 off-plan apartments that we had bought and sold to investors. With these coming up for completion I was close to achieving the goal of getting into the Rich List. Based on profit forecast, this hardly seemed like an issue. I was close, so close, but not quite there yet. I would have to bide just a little more time.

12

And the Walls Came Tumbling Down

The year 2008 was going to be the big one. I had acquired several off-plan blocks of apartments which often came with a two- to three-year build programme. It just so happened that the majority were scheduled to complete in 2008. This was going to be a bumper year of profits. I had been able to grow my business rapidly because I worked the model of empowerment, training others to do what I did. Finding the right people to train up was easy. They were the small-time investors who would initially pick up one or two off-plan apartments from me. And then came the chat. Why not scale up, why not buy several apartments from me and find buyers from your networks to buy from you?

Why not build up a host of mini-mes who thought like me and talked like me? The lure of buying more apartments from me to sell on was too much once the early taste had been a good one. Within a few years, some of my investors had built a large enough network to take fifty apartments off me at a time.

I saw it as empowering people to make good choices. And buying from me was certainly a good choice. What I did, they replicated. There were different sales methods in the trade but what we opted for was the "personal touch". Let's be honest, who would be stupid enough to buy property from telesales? Yes, people did it, but if you wanted real results you couldn't beat getting to know who you wanted to sell to. That was the difference between selling one and selling a hundred. Old school maybe, but it worked. Isn't it true that we all hate call centres because they are so fake? Yet we live with them because we have no choice. You see, nothing could beat the personal touch of making friends and mixing it with business. I was where I was because I had empowered others who in turn were empowering others!

This was certainly going to be my year, but I had no inkling of what was to come. As we moved into January, my property business, which was dependent on investors being able to complete their transactions, suddenly ground to a halt as the mortgage market collapsed. It happened fast and it was brutal with no time to prepare or plan. The tap was turned off and the next twenty-four months were to be the most testing time of my life. As a company, we were left holding hundreds of millions of pounds-worth of property contracts, and as each block came to completion we were left in the firing line as many of our investors simply couldn't complete on the properties they had exchanged contracts on.

I had no idea how I was going to get through this. I was sinking fast and there was no respite. I was trapped in a chain. The developers were under pressure from their banks and the banks were under pressure to get their hands on as much money as they could. Values had plummeted overnight and the whole thing was a complete and utter mess. Without bank finance, the trading model my business utilized could not operate. All these contracts that we had spent years researching, acquiring, and selling were now totally defunct. All those twelve-hour days of sailing close to the wind and all those nights when I couldn't sleep because I was trying to work out how I was going to sell the next block would now come to nothing.

Over the course of the next two years I found myself in and out of hospital with regular anxiety attacks when my body would suddenly seize up and I would struggle to breathe. What had I done to my family? I had thought I was invincible. I had refused to believe even a recession could halt the progress of my company. I was wrong. The crunch had turned our world upside down, leaving both our business and personal finances in tatters. Over those two years I would find myself sitting in front of one developer after another as we tried to find a way of making the best of a bad lot. Any value in the business would soon go as the developers, like vultures, took whatever they could. Some developers became darker in their dealings. Polite business talk turned into threatening phone calls and hints at what would come if I failed to find them their money.

I had built my whole world around money. That is where I had put my security. When that was gone, what would be left? On 8 January 2009, an article appeared in *The Guardian* called "The masters of the universe who cannot live with failure" by Andrew Clark, which described how many high-profile businessmen were driven to take their lives as a result of the sudden slumps in their fortunes and status. The article (which can be found on http://www.theguardian.com/business/2009/jan/08/credit-crunch-suicide) described how billionaire industrialist and Germany's fifth richest man, Adolf Merckle, threw himself under a train, how French fund manager Thierry de la Villehuchet was found dead, his arms slit, at his desk in New York, how San Francisco hedge fund manager Eric Von der Porten killed himself after his fund dropped by more than 40 per cent, and in Britain how fund management boss Kirk Stephenson jumped in front of a train after struggling with the financial crisis' impact on his company. In the article, Lanny Berman, executive director of the American Association of Suicidology, said that because some people's sense of self is so dependent on their concept of success, failure led them very quickly into a state of despair. And Ronald Maris, director of the University of South Carolina's suicide research centre, further added that they've got more to lose – the change in lifestyle, the disruption and suddenness of it. And of course there were many others who lost their money and their lives.

The credit crunch was to dramatically change my life both at work and at home. It was a huge shock to the system. Whereas before I had gone on expensive business lunches, I now found myself holding meetings over tea in motorway service stations. At our 2007 Christmas bash we had spent approximately £15,000 entertaining our best clients at a London restaurant. The following year would be a modest meal for four in a local eatery. Luxurious family holidays in hotel suites in Dubai and Mauritius would be replaced with less pricey breaks in a cottage or caravan in the UK. Instead of purchasing tailored clothing I now found myself scouring the high street for bargains. The scale of the change both at work and at home would take some getting used to. However, as one significant event unfolded I became less concerned with my own life and circumstance. This event would put the credit crunch into perspective when I encountered its full force.

My son, Ishaan, had just turned two. He had severe asthma and had been hospitalized on a number of occasions with life-threatening breathing difficulties. In February 2008, his condition suddenly worsened and my wife took him to the doctors as his breathing became more laboured. When the nurse practitioner saw him, she immediately called for an ambulance. At Northwick Park Hospital he was rushed into Accident and Emergency, where they quickly proceeded to administer the nebulizer. With this failing to work and with Ishaan's breathing rapidly deteriorating, he was rushed into resuscitation where several medical staff, including doctors, appeared within seconds.

Amidst the turmoil, Ishaan had stopped breathing and was intubated to keep him alive. The insertion of the flexible plastic tube into the trachea provided a means of mechanical ventilation, as the doctors toiled for a number of hours to bring Ishaan to some form of stability. There were clearly lots of complications, such as his carbon dioxide levels. Everything was moving at such a fast pace, and Maria and I faced the possibility we might lose our child. During the commotion, I remember noticing beads of sweat forming on the medical staff as we were ushered into a nearby room. I gained some comfort in seeing one nurse in the team who had attended to Ishaan on a previous occasion when he was hospitalized. The nurses we encountered had always been great but this one looked after my child like he was her own, like there was a deeper connection. I can't explain it, but I was thankful she was there.

Now that I was up against it, and completely powerless to help, I turned to God. The last time I had prayed properly was probably on that hockey pitch over twenty years before. In recent years, I had made money and success my god. But at this point all the money in the world wouldn't make a blind bit of difference. In the room next to the resuscitation theatre, the only option we had was going to God. Fear gripped me as I reflected on the way I had been living my life. Was this my comeuppance? Was this all my fault? Nonetheless, we prayed in desperation. I had pushed God away only to be coming back when I needed Him. As we prayed, I recall feeling that same presence that I had encountered back at Cavina School in Kenya. It had been a long time since I had felt it but I recognized it immediately. God was here. We had called and He had come.

After a considerable amount of time, the medical staff got Ishaan to a stable enough condition. The Children's Acute Transport Service was contacted and Ishaan was transferred to the Evelina ward at St Thomas's Hospital in London. I vividly recall one of the doctors looking extremely distressed. With tears in her eyes, she stated that they had been so close to losing Ishaan. We didn't know what the future held for him, but the medical staff had certainly done the best they could.

At St Thomas's, Ishaan was wired up to all kinds of machinery and tubes. My wife and I wept uncontrollably at his bedside. As the doctors attended to Ishaan, what became apparent was that he had had infections which had probably caused the previous hospitalizations. I was known for being insensitive and ruthless but seeing my critically ill son was tearing me apart. I remember going for a walk one day in the hospital and finding myself outside a chapel. As I wept there, I again felt the presence that I had felt in Cavina and at

Northwick Park Hospital as the medics had fought for my son's life.

On the fourth day, the consultant calmly spoke to my wife and me. She told us that Ishaan, though stable, had gone through a huge trauma, and hence we should not expect him to open his eyes for some time yet. It appeared to be one of those talks that was aimed at preparing us for the worst, just in case Ishaan's condition were to deteriorate. I owned a successful property business and a comfortable home, yet I would have given it all away in return for seeing Ishaan open his eyes. At the same time, my wife and I felt immensely touched by the prayers of a Christian couple we had recently befriended. My daughter, Chandni, had made friends with Marci and Nick's daughter and I was hugely touched by Marci's constant phone calls and by her getting her contacts in America to pray for Ishaan. I remember being broken by the compassion of this woman for my child. We didn't know her very well and so I couldn't get my head round the fact that she was constantly asking for updates. It didn't make any sense to me. They hardly knew us. Why would their family in America pray for my son when they had never met him? In my Hindu upbringing I had never experienced praying together as a whole family for others. Maybe my father and mother prayed for people outside our family, but I had never publicly witnessed it. Why then would a lady called Marci who hardly knew us be so hurt by the suffering we were going through?

After hearing the update from the consultant, I reflected on the love of Marci. The consultant had said Ishaan wouldn't be opening his eyes yet. But, I somehow felt strengthened by the prayers of our new friends. With all this resonating in my mind, on that fourth day as the consultant did her ward round, Ishaan suddenly bolted upright in bed and immediately began pulling away at the wires and tubes. What joy. What tears of joy. He was alive. My son was alive!

We had witnessed a miracle. God had come and my son's eyes were open. After all the elation, I recall turning to Maria and saying to her that once things were settled, we would most certainly go as a family to our friends' church to say thank you to them and to "their God". After experiencing the incredible compassion of Marci and Nick for my son, and seeing his dramatic recovery, this was the least that I could do. In my heart I knew I needed to do this, and nothing was going to stop me from keeping the promise I had made to myself.

13

Light

============

Maria was utterly shocked by my suggestion to visit the church. During the years Maria and I had been together, we had seldom talked about God. There had been one particular occasion one year when Maria had suggested it would be nice to attend a Christmas service, to which I had responded with such hostility that she never mentioned the idea again.

We visited Marci's church for two consecutive weeks. It felt good to be in a sacred space to thank God for what He had done for my family. Having shown my gratitude, I had no plans to go back the third week. However, Marci contacted us to say that they were visiting another church in Watford the following Sunday, and asking if we wanted to tag along. Not wishing to appear rude, I agreed. So we turned up at Soul Survivor, which was part of the Church of England, but not the typical kind of church. It was based in an industrial estate and operated out of a warehouse. As we entered this unusual church building, I instantly felt a presence. I later listened with interest to the sermon and the contemporary Christian songs. I liked it so much that to my surprise I decided I wanted to go back again.

Over the coming Sundays I was moved by the passion and elation of the vibrant congregation as they worshipped God. As I eagerly observed the joyous expressions of those around me, I began to grow in the awareness that God was not only real but intimate. And before I knew it, I had opened my mouth and joined in the singing. As I started singing songs of worship something started to stir within me. I couldn't put my finger on it, but I knew I was encountering something. The feeling was like the one I had had at Cavina – a sense of something greater, grander. At Cavina I had felt alive, and here once again I was experiencing a similar sensation. It felt like God was meeting with me as I offered songs of praise.

In all my time at Soul Survivor I never felt I was preached at. No one tried to convince me to believe in anything. I came because in that place I found peace and joy. And how was I to know that one evening I would proceed to walk to the front of the room when the congregation was asked if anyone would like to give their life to Jesus? And how was I to know that as I knelt down and two men prayed for me, that the last thirty-six years of my life would whiz past me in a millisecond, and as I would open my eyes, tears would be streaming down my face as I experienced the overwhelming love of God wash over me? In that single moment my world and my life completely changed. I recall opening my eyes and noticing everything looked different. I was seeing the world with new eyes. It was as if I had been seeing the world through a hazy microscope but now that I had accepted Jesus into my life, everything was in clear focus.

Over the coming weeks I was utterly broken by the cross of Jesus. I was broken by a God who had died for me so that I could have life. I had seen the cross many times on church buildings and as jewellery around people's necks, a symbol I knew well. But now the cross took on deeper significance. I had done so many bad things in my life. God knew my history and it was steeped in sin. I should have been standing in front of God in judgment, and yet in accepting Jesus Christ as my saviour I was experiencing not judgment but forgiveness. I spent most Sundays weeping at the foot of the cross. Why did He do it? Why had He been prepared to be whipped, beaten, tortured, abused, mocked, and nailed to a cross? Why had He suffered for the sake of no-hopers like me?

Maria didn't recognize me after I had become a Christian. One of the first things I said to her was "sorry". She had not heard me say this word for several years, but I would now be using it regularly! In accepting Jesus I had invited Him into my life, to take residency in me, to work in my life and shape me into the man He wanted me to be. I knew I would never quite get there this side of heaven. I would always be a bit of a mess, but with Jesus in my life I had the potential to be a better person than I currently was. For Maria and me, it was like starting over again and getting to know one another for the first time. I later read about the apostle Paul in the Bible who had lived a pretty bad life in persecuting Christians. But then one day he was on the road to Damascus and encountered Jesus. Following that meeting, Paul was a different man. No longer was he persecuting followers of Jesus, but instead telling other people about Him. Like Paul, I had experienced an all-singing-all-dancing transformation. I had gone to church one day as one man, and come out as another. In seeing the change that was taking place in me, Maria's faith suddenly came back to life. Deep down she had always believed, and now her faith had been reignited.

Yet, I hadn't been looking for God. Rather, throughout my life the God of the Bible had been chasing me. I didn't choose Jesus but Jesus chose me. Clearly, at Cavina School over twenty years prior I had felt my heart stirred with the presence of something greater. But that was a long time ago, and indeed so much had happened since then. I had gone to secondary school in Kenya, before attending a boarding school back in England. I had then travelled extensively, before going on to university in North Wales. Following three years of higher education, I briefly moved to Nottingham, then Wandsworth for the next five years before moving closer to my roots in Watford. Many years had elapsed, but as I came home one day after a Sunday service, I looked at the bookshelf in my room and to my utter disbelief noticed a copy of the Bible, a Book of Common

Prayer, a book of hymns, and an autobiography of the evangelist George Whitefield staring back at me. Suddenly, I recollected that these were the books I possessed at Cavina. How could it be possible that they were still with me? I was notorious for chucking things out. Yet, to my utter astonishment, the only items that I still retained from my time in Kenya, some twenty years prior, were the four books on my shelf. For a moment, I convinced myself that these books must indeed have been most precious to me to have packed them when I left Kenya. However, over time it began to dawn upon me that the packing of these books had nothing to do with me. The reality wasn't that I had deemed these books precious, but rather that God deemed me precious. Yes, God had been chasing me all those years.

Some years after being a follower of Jesus, I was invited to a local church in Watford to share my story of coming to faith. Here I met a lady who happened to have gone to Cavina School. As we talked, she explained how her missionary father was part of a group of school parents who came together to pray for the students in the school. At the time when I was at Cavina, her father, Mike Power, had put me on his weekly prayer list. I was shocked to discover that some twenty-five years later, I was still on his weekly prayer list! God had been at work all those years ago and stirred Mike and others to pray regularly for me and my salvation. I have no idea who else must have been praying for me to come to faith, but I suspect somebody was.

As you can imagine, my new-found faith in Jesus came as a surprise to friends and family. Indeed, for many, the decision to "convert" from one's family religion can be very costly, and I have often taken for granted being in the enviable position of having very thoughtful and understanding parents. Although when I was a child, my father in particular had been opposed to me following Jesus, now he graciously allowed me to express this decision as an adult, without complaint. In part this was no doubt because as followers of Hinduism, my parents accepted Christianity as one of the many pathways to God. The Hindu worldview can lead to a wonderfully embracing nature that sees the good in all the main faiths, and I admire my mother and my father for visiting my church on many occasions, sometimes even bringing members of her family along with her. It means a lot to me that despite our differing opinions, my parents and I are able to respect one another's choices and love one another in them.

In June 2014 I was at a Christian conference where I listened with interest as a lady called Ness Wilson talked about a story in the Bible about a man called Jairus. He was well regarded in the community, a man of good standing. But this man throws himself in desperation before Jesus when his daughter is ill. This man is so public with his helplessness. With nowhere else to go, Jairus publicly falls at the feet of Jesus. This is a story of a high-powered individual saying to God, "I need You; I am a person in need of Jesus."

Like Jairus, I had come to the end of my own resou
when my son was ill, and like Jairus, I too fell at the
feet of Jesus.

Listening to Ness was a profound day for me.
Following the talk she asked us to close our eyes and
to picture ourselves wearing robes. But I felt God
inviting me to come to Him without the robes, so that
He could dust me down, clean me up, and give me
rest. In coming to Jesus that day in 2008 I had brought
before Him my role, my title, my gifts. I had taken
off my robe, my achievements, my accomplishments.
I had laid aside determination, competition, and
jealousy, and instead I invited Jesus to take their place.
In making a commitment I became a son of God. All
these years I had been trying to live outside of the love
of God when in fact He was calling me to be His child.
I was learning that being a child of God was not some
theological phrase, but our identity. We are so deeply
loved. No matter what roles we have, and how we are
perceived, we are just His children.

Since coming to faith in Jesus, I have listened to many
talks but that day listening to Ness was particularly
relevant to me. I needed reminding that God was my
Father and I was His child. In the meditation I saw a
picture of God combing my hair, like a parent combs
a child's hair. As I left His presence I was handed the
comb, being asked to do likewise to others. This is
what Marci had been doing in praying for Ishaan. She
was able to love because God loved her first.

to write an honest version of this
point of view.

Marci's story

only just arrived in the UK from Florida
and were bringing our daughter to the first day of
school when I met Maria. We made eye contact on
the sidewalk and exchanged a little nervous laughter
and some pleasantries about it being the first day and
how we were more nervous than the children. I liked
her right away. Over the next short weeks, we began
a new friendship. We visited each other's homes for
dinner with the families a few times, and got together
for a cup of tea while the girls were in school. The
girls became friends and the hubbies got along as
well. Manoj was immediately likeable. He had a great
sense of humour, was genuinely interested in who we
were and what our experience in the UK had been
like thus far. Through our conversations, and maybe
some Googling, we learnt that Maria and Manoj had
experienced an impressive level of success and that
Manoj was an ambitious businessman. This explained
the large home, the luxury car, the expensive clothes.

Manoj was not arrogant in a way that would make
you dislike him. He seemed confident and energized
by his success. Business seemed of the utmost
importance to him. I know at that time, he worked
long hours away from his family and had managed to
provide a very comfortable life for them.

My friendship with Maria was based on mutual
silliness, really. I have never laughed more with
a girlfriend than I did and do with her! I knew

something about her background, that she had been raised Pentecostal, but that since marrying Manoj, had not been a churchgoing Christian. I sensed that she missed practising her faith. Manoj described himself as Hindu, with "a little h".

I received a message from Maria that her son had been taken ill because of his severe asthma, that they were at the hospital with Ishaan and that he was on a ventilator. For me, I was immediately brought to tears and all I knew at that point was that I needed to talk to my friend. I took that chance that she would answer and called her mobile. The sound of pure desperation and fear in her voice was unmistakable. The only help I could offer her was prayer. She was my friend and her family was in desperate need of comfort and a miracle. I believe we prayed right there on the phone. I told her that I would call my mother in the US and that she would have her church lift up Ishaan in prayer. I also said that I would contact the church we had left recently in Florida and have them pray. Given the time difference between the UK and the US, I left messages with both my mother and friend at the church. They both confirmed that they would get the prayer groups to pray that very morning. After leaving those messages, I didn't know what else to do but drop down and pray. As a mother, I could imagine the emotions that my friends were feeling and I knew that only God could grant them peace and work a miracle. I don't remember my words. I do remember that I was pleading. It didn't matter that Manoj wasn't a Christian, I was.

Maria later told me that just about the time that everyone began praying for Ishaan, he sat up in bed and wanted the ventilator out. I was just amazed. How incredible it was to see the power of prayer so quickly. After Ishaan returned home, Manoj wanted to visit our church to say thank you to God for saving his boy. I didn't really understand if he was curious about Jesus, or if he was interested in demonstrating to me that he was thanking God. Who was I to question his motives? Manoj shared with me that when he was younger, he had attended a Christian school and was curious about the faith. At that time, he didn't have the familial support necessary to explore that option and he had tabled his interest. Now, decades later, God was bringing about the change in Manoj that He had begun many years before.

Over the next months, Manoj became a man on fire for God. He fully and completely committed himself to Christ and to sharing the good news of Jesus with those who did not yet know Him. While his desires shifted from success in business, it was clear that his passion now lay in serving God. It was humbling to see Manoj's personality become so markedly changed. There was a humility there that wasn't there before. A gratefulness and an outward desire to know and please God became obvious character traits. I have no idea what it's like to change your faith from that of your family. I can imagine that it takes great strength and conviction. Manoj had that.

In the first year of being a follower of Jesus, I often sensed God my heavenly Father saying to me, "I heard those prayers of Marci, and I rescued your son, but Manoj, I always want you to remember that my son I did not rescue, my son Jesus went to the cross so that you can have new life." I marvelled at the immensity of God's love and grace (that is, His free, unmerited, unearned favour) for me.

This isn't a story about my performance and how I turned my life around. This is a story of Jesus' performance on the cross. I had put my faith in money, but all that paled into insignificance the day I gave my life to Jesus. In Jesus I had found real treasure, one that wouldn't tarnish, one that wouldn't be devalued by wayward markets; it was a priceless treasure that gave life and meaning.

14

Learning to Let Go

What ensued for a few weeks after I began to follow Jesus was an inner struggle. As I wavered, I began to wonder if the powerful experience I had had in the church that day when I first committed myself to Jesus was a figment of my imagination. Maybe it was all just in my mind. With these thoughts resonating in my head, I found myself randomly falling into conversation with a member of the congregation called Emmanuel. The result was that I reluctantly agreed to go to his midweek prayer group. His friendly persistence paid off and I had lost the urge to resist.

At the prayer meeting I was greeted by a room full of extremely kind-looking faces, who welcomed me as an old friend. However, the old Manoj was still holding on and I convinced myself that this was the last thing I needed. Here I was, giving up my precious time for a God who might not even exist, and worse still, I was surrounded by a group of people that clearly believed otherwise. Fortunately, Dean, the owner of the house, came to my rescue, diverting my awkwardness by putting on a CD of worship music. As the group joined in singing, I remember suddenly feeling filled with a deep sense of peace. The inner turmoil I had experienced for some days immediately vanished. I was so taken aback by the soothing impact of the music that I planned to ask Dean if I could borrow the CD. However, before I got the opportunity to do so, Dean suddenly walked over to me to give me the CD, stating that God had just told him that I wanted to borrow it and to give it to me. As you can imagine, I was utterly astounded.

That evening I briefly sat in the car before I made my way home. I was totally in awe of what I had just experienced. How had Dean known I wanted the CD? And then out of nowhere came a voice saying, "Do you still doubt Me?" I was totally overwhelmed as the presence of God filled the car. Any doubts I had had immediately melted away. I sat in the car for what seemed like ages in utter shock by what I had just experienced.

That night I entered the house with a completely new perspective. I had just witnessed the glory of God and it had totally blown me away. I felt drawn to go to the dining room. Here I noticed a photograph of my son at nursery, and seated near him was a young boy called Ethan. Only then did the penny drop. Ethan's father was Emmanuel, who had invited me to the prayer meeting. As I reflected on the evening's events, I realized that God was the great conductor, the only one who had a clear view of the different ensembles. I'd had no idea that

Ethan's parents went to the same church as us. I had never seen them at the nursery. Unbeknown to me, God had used Emmanuel to draw me back to Him. Seeing the picture of Ethan confirmed that God was always at work. God had given me another sign to cement that He was real. That day, my knowledge of God's grace was profoundly enhanced. Despite the fact that He had saved my son and I had wavered, I realized that the door was always open. Through the encounter with Emmanuel and Dean, God was encouraging me to come back to Him. The choice was clearly mine. God was not going to pressure me. But how could I resist? God's grace was simply too good to turn down. That night I lay prostrate on my dining room floor recommitting my life to Him.

Over the course of the following weeks, I steadily grew in my faith and the knowledge that God's grace took care of the issue of sin so that I could walk freely into His presence. But what I hadn't envisaged was that by this process, I would in a sense be "elevated". My life was truly turning around. Over the course of my life I had been self-destructing without being aware of it. Like a puzzle, God was putting the pieces of my complex, broken life back together again. He was restoring relationships. Where there was pain and hurt, God was bringing healing. I was like a damaged sculpture being carefully restored back to its original design.

As I deeply reflected on the course of my life, what dawned upon me was that I had been focusing on the things I thought were important but failed to focus on the things that were truly important! I had allowed my life to become skewed. For many years it had been financial success I had given significance to, it was living in a nice house I had given significance to, it was being recognized as successful by others that I had given significance to. I thought I was living but I only really started living when God in His grace turned up and showed me a different way. At the time of writing I am forty-two years old and I could say I have been living for forty-two years. But in my heart I know I have only been living since 2008. What I thought was significant before paled into insignificance when I met Jesus.

Some years after the experience above, a verse in the book of Philippians in the Bible deeply resonated with me: "Indeed, I count everything as loss because of the surpassing worth of knowing Christ Jesus my Lord" (3:8, ESV).

The reality is that I could have enjoyed a life with Jesus much sooner. I had come to know about Him at Cavina School but it took some twenty-five years of living a messy life before making a commitment. The thing that had been stopping me was letting go of control. When it came to passing the buck on mundane things that had to be done, I was happy with that. But when it came to major decision-making, I had to be in charge. I had the idea that if I wanted something done properly I had to be in the driving seat. The truth of the matter was that my driving ability was causing a pile-up in my life. In travelling with Jorgen many years previously, I recall how I had enjoyed that moment in Cannes on the beach where I surrendered to the sun and the heat. It was in the letting go I could have found freedom in Jesus and freedom from myself. If only I had worked that out sooner.

Recently I watched the *Life of Pi*. As Pi reflects on his life and the struggles of being shipwrecked and surviving 227 days on a lifeboat in the Pacific Ocean he says that the journey of life becomes a process of letting go. For him, the whole of life became an act of surrender. And it was through letting go that I myself encountered the grace of God. It was through saying, "I can't earn my salvation" that I found peace. It was through coming to that point when I said, "Not my way but Your way" that I found life's true meaning. I had begun to understand what Jesus meant when he said, "For whoever would save his life will lose it, but whoever loses his life for my sake will find it" (Matthew 16:25, ESV).

The *Life of Pi*, according to author Yann Martel, reveals that a life with God is a better story. And yet for much of my life, a story with God had hardly seemed the better story. We are called to live not with grasping fists but with open hands: how else can we receive a gift but with open hands? And what greater gift can God give than Himself?

Accepting God's grace had not been easy for me. It had meant accepting that I was a sinner, and who wants to admit to that? It meant saying that I needed help; again, who wants to admit to that? It meant saying I couldn't earn my own salvation, even though at times I believed I had the ability to be godly in my own strength. Christianity seemed to be a cop-out, the religion for those who couldn't be bothered to make an effort. It was the religion that said you could be completely forgiven by accepting what Jesus has done on the cross for you. It is not surprising, therefore, that Jesus said that if you want to enter the kingdom of heaven you must become childlike with humble and sincere hearts (see Matthew 18:2–4). Whereas children accept, adults question. Undoubtedly I needed to learn to really let go if I was to truly benefit from this new life in Jesus. Thankfully, help would come from an unlikely source.

15

Guided by the Holy Spirit

W hen I committed to Jesus, I didn't do so out of having wrestled with the basis of the Christian faith or through academic study. It just happened. Unbeknown to me, God had been at work in my life for many years, and following Ishaan's survival, my turning to Jesus was quick. My lack of biblical knowledge therefore meant I found myself pretty much learning on the job, and one area that took getting used to was how I felt after giving my life to Jesus. After relinquishing control that day at Soul Survivor church, I immediately felt different, like there was something alive and clean inside me. It was a totally wonderful new sensation.

In a sense I had committed to Jesus without really knowing what following Him entailed. There were a number of changes happening to my nature, not by my own doing but by God's. Suddenly I found I was growing in compassion for others and that relationships were being strengthened, and that the love of money was diminishing as my passion to tell everyone about Jesus was increasing. I surely must have put a few people off following Jesus in the early days, as I shared my excitement about my new-found faith, and I know that this was sometimes a bit much for close family. Ironically, at the charismatic church in Bangor many years before I had thought the congregation were strange but that was because I wasn't in their position of having experienced the joy of Christ. Although I could understand that God was at work reshaping my character and my outlook, what I couldn't understand was the new feeling I had inside of me. Gradually I learnt that when a person commits their life to Jesus they receive the Spirit, the Holy Spirit, who lives in them and transforms them from the inside. Through the Holy Spirit, God's love is poured into their hearts. Two incidents early on in my new faith helped me to comprehend a bit more of what was going on inside me.

The first encounter was when I was walking through Euston station one day with a book of some sort under my arm – I can't remember what it was – at rush hour. Crowds of people were bustling past me when I walked by a man who was collecting money for some charity and I suddenly felt a voice telling me to turn around. As I did so, the voice told me to give the book to the man, so I went up to him. Before I had even had time to explain who I was, he put his hand on my forehead as if he was expecting me. He proceeded to bless me and say that there were not many of us, meaning Christians. The encounter lasted only a few seconds, with me then giving him the book which he readily accepted as if he was expecting it. As I continued on my journey I was left with a number of questions. Who was this person? Where had the voice come from to tell me to turn around? How did he know I was a Christian? Why was I meant to give him the book?

In time I came to realize that this voice inside me was the Holy Spirit, God's presence transforming me and guiding me. I didn't hear any audible voice as such; it was more of a strong impression, prompting my action. I later came across a verse in the Bible that says, "Do not neglect to show hospitality to strangers, for thereby some have entertained angels unawares" (Hebrews 13:2, ESV). Without my knowing these words, I was being guided to the right actions. The whole incident had seemed so surreal and yet there was a real spiritual presence there.

A second incident happened soon after this when I was on the train one day. The carriage was packed and I was eating a bag of crisps when I suddenly felt a strong impression that I was to offer out the crisps to my fellow passengers. With the sensation not leaving, I proceeded to offer out the crisps. On London trains, people are usually heads down reading the *Evening Standard*, with eye contact forbidden and disrupting anyone with a smile or conversation the ultimate sin! But one man responded and we got chatting. Before I knew it, I was sharing about my faith and he was explaining how his faith had gone to sleep. As I described my experiences

I could see he was deeply moved, and he said that he felt I had been sent to him to nudge him to return to a faith in God. As I left the train, he shook my hand in gratitude with tears in his eyes. Again all I had been doing was responding to that quiet voice inside me. Over time I came to appreciate the work of the Holy Spirit in helping Christians to play their part in God's overarching plan to draw others into an intimate relationship with Him. Often I would ignore the voice because I was caught up in the busyness of this world, whereas at other times I would be sensitive to the Holy Spirit, and sometimes I would get all mixed up thinking it was God when actually it was my own thoughts.

Much later I came across another verse in the Bible, about the Holy Spirit: "Do you not know that your bodies are temples of the Holy Spirit, who is in you, whom you have received from God? You are not your own; you were bought at a price" (1 Corinthians 6:19–20, NIV).

In having received the Holy Spirit, I began to appreciate that I belonged to God. I was no longer the boss of my life and the Holy Spirit was there to guide me in serving Him by helping others. For example, some while back when I was on holiday, my family and I happened to stop at an idyllic church fair. Inside was a fantastic array of embroidery, artwork, and homeware. As I wandered around the stalls, my eye was drawn to a small cushion. Though beautifully stitched, it looked subdued compared to its larger, colourful neighbours. I decided, to the amazement of my family, to buy the cushion. Back at the holiday home, I discovered that the maker's name was tagged on to the cushion. I felt this overwhelming desire to pray for the lady who had made the cushion. As I prayed, a picture formed in my mind of a woman who had been blessed with the ability to use her hands to create, but was suffering with a bone condition that was impacting on her life. Without any evidence, I asked Maria to pray for the woman who had made the cushion.

Later that night, Maria told me how she felt God had shown her that there was a lady in her fifties who was suffering with a bone condition. Together we were able to lift her up in prayer for God to help in her time of need.

Before our holiday ended, we decided to pop back to the craft fair to purchase some more cushions in the same fabric. We were delighted to meet the lady who had made the cushions. As we talked with her, she briefly explained that she had recently been diagnosed with an illness which affected her bones.

When I reflect on this day, I remember that I was more relaxed than I normally am. Often people say that in these quieter, calmer moments we can hear more clearly from God. God wants to be in conversation with us about all sorts of things and about all sorts of people, if only we can be more still. Having bought additional cushions, I have been able to place these at home and at my workplace, thus encouraging me to pray for her frequently.

Another truth that I learnt about the Holy Spirit was that now I was no longer alone. God was with me; God had come near. The Holy Spirit is personal, God living in us. There would be times of trial ahead and God wouldn't always take the pain away, but He was the great comforter, just as Jesus had promised His followers He would be, in John's Gospel.

Some time ago, when I was exploring the role of the Holy Spirit, I came across a quote by a famous Christian called A. W. Tozer. He said he wanted the presence of God, and did not want anything to do with religion. He didn't want a social club. He wanted everything God had, or nothing!

I quickly realized that in having been given His Holy Spirit, it was up to me whether I accessed His presence or not. It was up to me whether I chose to depend on and listen to the Holy Spirit or not. It was a matter of choice. I have since found that when I do so I am a much better person and more in tune with what God wants me to do. At other times busyness takes over and God gets displaced.

Tozer's quote helped me to appreciate that there were different degrees of Christianity I could opt for. I could call myself a Christian and go to church but the rest of the week live a life devoid of the presence of God, live as if I was still "my own". And how often I have done that! Like a time when I was with my twin sister and tried to cram more people in the back of the car than there was space for, only for her to say that it was against the law. Sure, it was only for a very short journey, but she was right. I had parked my Christianity at church that Sunday.

Over time I have come to realize that listening is key to the outworking of the Holy Spirit. I recall one friend, Bridget Adams, who combined being a business consultant with being a vicar in the Church of England, and with whom I would eventually set up a company. She always paused during our conversations as if to listen to what the Holy Spirit was saying, something that made her a good person to talk to when faced with a dilemma, because she had created a lifelong attitude to listening. But listening has never been my forte and I admire my mother-in-law, Georgina, for her ability to do so. This became plainly evident during a time when my son was proving to be very difficult to get into bed because he was obsessed about needing the blanket to be ultra-neat without a single crease. As you can imagine, bedtimes were extremely testing, trying to settle my son down, because it was almost impossible to get him in bed without causing some crease on the blanket. This went on for weeks until one day Georgina phoned to ask if Ishaan was struggling with going to sleep because of this particular issue. We had not told Georgina anything about it, but God had informed her, and as a result she was able to talk to my wife, and give her advice. Soon after, Ishaan stopped having issues with bedtime. It wasn't that my mother-in-law was some "super-Christian", just simply that she chose to spend time with God in prayer and learnt to recognize His voice.

Receiving the Holy Spirit transformed my life. I had been living outside of God all those years, missing out on intimacy. Now I had received the Holy Spirit, I had the presence of God the Most High with me throughout each day and each night. But the Holy Spirit was more than some power to draw on to speak into the lives of others: He was also there to work in my own life, and sometimes this proved to be very challenging indeed.

16

The Honest Cost of Sin

n coming to faith, one of the first things that God alerted me to was my lack of honesty, and over the years I had stored up many dark secrets in my life. I had started life as an innocent child but over the course of time transformed into the antithesis of innocence. I had given into temptation again and again, with the love of money playing a large part in this. It had changed me, it had deformed me, and it had led me down a self-destructive path. Money had influenced my motives and my desires: I had elevated it above all other things and placed myself firmly outside the camp of God, and suffered the consequences. A lot of people used to say, "You are a good guy, Manoj!", but I knew my hidden past, the truth. Being honest with myself was difficult because it meant accepting what I was really like, and I cringe at the thought of how I was before becoming a Christian. I regret so much and I wish I could turn back time, yet I realize that God somehow has the ability to use the wrong we do to bring some good.

The reality is that even though I have decided to follow Jesus, I still make mistakes, I still cringe, though not in the same way I once did. Believing in Jesus hasn't made me perfect, but it does mean I am forgiven and have the freedom to change.

For me, being honest has been liberating. I was weighed down by the things of the past, the huge regrets, and in coming to Jesus these "chains" were removed. In coming to God and acknowledging my sins I received forgiveness, a new start, a previously unknown peace and joy, and the privilege of playing a small part in His overall story, which has given me incredible purpose and meaning. I was born for relationship with Jesus and I had found no real satisfaction outside of Him, but with Him everything made sense and, like any good relationship, honesty would be key.

Ultimately I managed to be honest with God because, at the end of the day, He already knew everything about me – and had promised to love me. However bad I had been, I could rely on God to forgive me. That's just His nature; He can't help it. He forgives and remembers sin no more.

What I found more difficult was being honest with others. The question was, would they also be able to forgive me?

Shortly after beginning a part-time course at St Mellitus College, I felt the Holy Spirit challenging me one day to greater honesty with others. I tried to brush it aside but throughout that day at the college and on my way home, this feeling just wouldn't go away. I felt like a pressure cooker without a release valve, apart from that which I knew God was asking me to do – to be honest about my past with Maria. God warned me as I prayed about it that there would be pain, but I also felt that if I was obedient things would somehow be OK. The thing is, being honest with my wife was the last thing I wanted to do. Wasn't it enough that I had given my life to the Lord? Couldn't my past just be our secret? Maria and I had been together for such a long time, five years before we got married, and at this time we had been married for seven years. All marriages have their problems, with highs and lows, laughter and tears, and we had gone through a lot in twelve years. Was I prepared to potentially lose my marriage for the sake of honesty? The reality was that I had been a terrible husband, but in Maria I had found a beautiful person both on the inside and outside. You just don't often meet people like her. She had a sincerity and purity about her, and had worked hard not to be influenced by the ways of the world, by bitterness, jealousy, and greed. God had blessed me with the ultimate wife! Time and time again people would comment on how lovely she was. How could I have been so foolish to betray her trust so many times? What would Maria think of me? Would she even want to be with me? Why would I risk the break-up of our marriage just for the sake of being honest about things now in the past?

But God reassured me again and again that He would heal, and in the end I knew I had to trust and obey Him. It wasn't easy having that conversation when I got home, and telling Maria that I hadn't always been faithful to her. It was difficult to tell her that I hadn't always been the person she had hoped I was, that all her fears had been justified. Some people had put me on a pedestal because of my achievements in the business and entertainment worlds, but I didn't want that any more. The brutal truth was that I was simply a wretched sinner who made my beautiful Maria cry that day. She didn't deserve this. No, not her, she didn't deserve this, and she didn't deserve me. How I regret my sinful past!

There is a verse in the book of Isaiah in the Bible when the prophet sees God and this immediately turns his attention to his own sinful nature. And this is what happened to me. Like the prophet, it was only when I came closer to God that I suddenly became aware of my own failings. For many years the cross had been an empty symbol on church buildings but now I realized what the cross stood for. God was holy, and I was not. And the way for me to be connected was the cross: the cross was the bloodied and precious bridge that healed the relationship.

God was faithful to His word. He had asked me to walk down this road of honesty and He was with us: I had been obedient, and healing began quickly. Maria forgave me instantly. I wanted her to rage at me, to go cold and shout at me, but she never did. She forgave me just like that, as Jesus forgave me. No bitterness, no anger. God had shown Maria a different way, the way of forgiveness. On the cross, Jesus had been humiliated and tortured. Before this He had performed miracles and He had healed the sick. Yet He chose on that day not to perform miracles; He chose on that day to bear the punishment for sin. Along with Him, a criminal was being crucified, a man who believed in Jesus. When He called out to Christ, Jesus forgave Him, saying, "today you will be with me in paradise" (Luke 23:43, NIV). And on that cross, Jesus even forgave the people who nailed Him there, saying, "Father, forgive them, for they do not know what they are doing" (Luke 23:34, NIV). And having received Jesus in her life, this is what Maria was able to do now for me: forgive.

As a husband, I am still very much a work in progress. For years I had allowed so many bad habits to take ownership of my character, from arrogance to an extreme lack of patience. Over the course of the years, the Bible has challenged my view on how I should behave, particularly in the area of my marriage to Maria, showing me that I am called to love her as Jesus loves His people, the church. I earnestly seek to do this, but unfortunately I still have many terrible traits which God continues to chip away at. It is worrying, what happened to me without God in my life – it was dangerous and I was self-destructing, damaging those nearest and dearest to me. Yet healing has been made possible through honesty and forgiveness.

After I began to follow Jesus, I felt I wanted to recommit myself to Maria and renew our vows. It was a special day, just Maria, myself, a vicar, and his wife at a church in Wimbledon. It was an opportunity to invite God into our marriage, no longer for the two of us to be doing it alone, but with God at its centre in partnership with us. Since that day I find myself getting hugely disappointed when I hear of marriage break-ups and family breakdowns, because I know that they can be healed in Jesus. He is the great restorer and He does it so well. As we come to Him, we find that repair is possible. It breaks my heart to see people giving up when help is at hand; it is all restorable if only we will come.

Within the Asian community in which I have been raised, things often remain hidden so as not to bring shame to one's family. Problems tend to remain behind closed doors. By going public I know this will cause hurt to people near me, but I also know that it is sometimes important for the truth to be told so that others can find freedom and maybe avoid the same mistakes.

I really didn't want to write this chapter. Nobody really wants to tell the world how bad they have been, but in writing it I have realized again just how destructive sin is. It impacted not only my internal well-being but, worse than this, my wife and marriage. What's more, I had let Maria's mother down. How do you explain to a woman who has welcomed you into her home and given her daughter to you to care for and love that you have been unfaithful? But like Maria, Georgina forgave me. No questions, no anger. Just love and forgiveness. My head can't get round that conversation because it felt like Georgina was wondering why I was even asking her for forgiveness at all when she had already committed to loving me unconditionally.

It was with the encouragement of Maria, and God's promptings, that I wrote this chapter – without my wife's blessing I could never have shared it, for this is her story as well as mine, and making such things public after eighteen years of being together is no small thing. Maybe it will not show me in the best light, but if what I have written helps just one individual in coming to a place of honesty, it will so be worth it.

17

The Prince Family

It is often the case when one writes their story down that new issues surface with which one has to wrestle, and this has certainly been the case with this book. Recently I went for a long prayer walk to seek God's help in dealing with one particular matter that had come to light. Over time, I had gradually come to terms with Maria and Georgina's forgiving nature. Nonetheless, I was still struggling with having let Maria's wider family down. As I walked that day and prayed to God, He was to explain very clearly why I was feeling this way.

From the moment we first met, I was warmly accepted by the Prince family of Maria's six uncles and their respective families. As a child, Maria had lived for a while with her mother, siblings, grandparents, and six uncles in a three-bedroom house. They were a close-knit family and Maria has very fond memories of growing up in such a fun-filled and loving environment. One special memory is of her family gatecrashing her graduation ceremony. Although only two tickets were allocated, pretty much the whole family turned up. One way or another, they managed to get in and raucously celebrate Maria's achievements.

Since finding out about Georgina's vision that her daughter would marry an Indian man, I had been made to feel hugely welcome by the Prince family. When I became a Christian, I came to realize why God had orchestrated for me to be connected with this family. It was more than simply Maria and I being together; it ran much deeper than this. In being connected to the Prince family I was being connected to a strong line of believers in Jesus Christ.

Maria's grandfather was Christian Lewis Prince. He had had a huge experience of Jesus in his thirties and from that point onwards he had lived all-out for the good news of Jesus Christ. He understood the cross, he understood God's sacrifice for him, and it resonated so deeply that when he decided to follow Jesus he had committed to passionately serving God. He did this by preaching in churches, going on mission trips back to his homeland of St Kitts and Nevis and later to Jamaica. Together with his wife, Edna, they would become a powerhouse for God, touching the lives of many people. Obediently they set up a small church called Holy Apostle Pentecostal Church and ministered to people through it.

Maria recalls how her grandfather each week baked the bread that would be shared at church in memory of Jesus being the Bread of Life. This bread would be shared in the service, symbolizing Jesus' body that was broken for all. Over time, Christian Lewis Prince grew in faith and spiritual gifts, spending much time playing his guitar and singing worship songs, reading the Bible and praying. He grew in intimacy in his relationship with God and heard from God in many ways, including through visions. As a leader of a church, he took his responsibility of serving others as Jesus had served him very seriously.

I never met Christian; sadly, he died when Maria was young. Thankfully, however, I did meet Edna. I clearly remember that at our first meeting Edna had got out the best china cups and proceeded to write my name in her little book so that she could pray for me. And I know she did. Through the number of challenging times that would follow in my life, I am sure I was carried through the storms in no small part by Edna's prayers.

Christian and Edna had a significant impact on their family. At the family's core there is such a goodness, something I don't know that they are aware of. But looking in from the outside I can see how they carry the goodness of their upbringing with them. Despite this, my wife believes that in many ways her wider family have never fully recovered from Christian's early death. The church he had started with his wife continued for a while, but sadly Edna was often ill and her work in that ministry had to come to an end. She may have suffered in her older age with dementia but God never left her. I recall Maria seeing Edna one time when she no longer recognized anyone. Maria had prayed that she would recognize her and God answered the prayer – not only was she able to recognize Maria but she also had a very meaningful conversation with her. That afternoon as Maria read Psalm 23 from the Bible, Edna was able to recite the verses off by heart.

As I prayer walked and considered how my unfaithfulness impacted the Princes, I began to realize another significant aspect of why I had been connected to this amazing family. History has a habit of repeating itself, and my grandfather on my dad's side had been a fascinating man of business. Though I never really knew him I had adopted many of his characteristics, such as taking impulsive risks in the hope of getting rich quick, a behavioural streak that had got him into trouble. But through my marriage, God had intervened to put a stop to this cycle of history being repeated. The reckless streak would have dominated my life and I would have passed down this and other undesirable traits to my offspring, but fortunately I encountered Jesus and while I was still joined to my family, God had also joined me to a new family with a dramatically different history – and future. The pattern of my life and that of future generations had been disrupted.

Like Christian Lewis Prince, I would also find faith in my thirties. God could have intervened earlier in my life, and in many ways that would have been easier for my wife. But by allowing me to sink lower and lower into sin, grace would be all the more special when I experienced it. That day, God highlighted that

Christian Lewis was my third grandfather. I never met him but I feel as if I knew him. Metaphorically, he had become my spiritual grandfather. He was passionate about God's saving grace on the cross, and I pray that the awe I have of this amazing act of God will never stop burning in me. Christian would serve the church and I too have chosen to serve God's church. And that is why I was hurting. This was not just any family my marital infidelity had affected. No, this was my family too; I had let my family down.

Over the following days, as I reflected on what God was showing me, He reminded me of what I had named my children when they were born. It was customary that they took on my first name as their middle name. This was done to track the family tree. In the case of my father, he had taken his father's and grandfather's first names as his middle names. But in addition to giving my children my first name, I had also given them the name of "Prince" as their other middle name. This act was highly unusual in my culture, but for some reason I had broken with tradition and given them my wife's maiden name as well. At the time I didn't understand the significance of my actions, but in hindsight I can see that God was doing a new thing. He was changing history, He was threading in a new line down my ancestry. Names are important – that is why many Christians name their children after strong biblical characters. Unbeknown to me I had assigned my children the Prince name because this new name also came with history, the history of a man and woman who knew the love of God and were able to reflect that love to others. It is my hope and prayer that in giving this name to my children that they too will grow up to know the immensity of God's love for them.

Christian Lewis died early, but God always continues what He has started and that day as I prayer walked I felt some of that responsibility being given to my wife and me. I don't know what it all will look like, but in our little way we hope we can make a difference to the lives of others.

Some months ago I saw a vision when someone prayed for me at church. It involved me being taken by God into a dark place. In the vision I saw a dark and densely populated wood and I was standing outside it in the light. I wondered what this dark place signified, the only comfort being that God would take me there. Writing about my sinful past has very much felt like that dark place. I have come to realize the extent to which sin corrupts, corrodes, and breaks. It destroys people and relationships. Often we are unaware of the far-reaching effects of sin but grace reaches further and thankfully, through this process, I now know more about my connection to the Prince family. Sometimes it is when we are on our knees that God gives a vision that brings new understanding and fresh hope.

One of the most difficult things I have found is learning to forgive myself. I struggle because often I understand the cross with head knowledge, my thoughts, as opposed to heart knowledge, my emotions. My sins – past, present, and future – were nailed to the cross once and for all. On the cross, death was defeated. I hear that, but it doesn't always sink in. Yet it is something I must learn to do and I ask God to show me how to do it. After all, as we read in the book of Romans, there is "no condemnation for those who are in Christ Jesus" (8:1, NIV).

I very much look forward to meeting Christian Lewis Prince one day in heaven. He was named "Christian" and he wore that name well. He ran the race exquisitely, even unto death.

18

Baptized into Relationship

n coming to faith in Jesus, I wrestled for a number of months about the question of other faiths. For many, all religions lead to God and it was certainly a view I adhered to for a long time – all the main faith groups seemed to include people with a genuine commitment to God and to say that one was superior to another seemed to be an arrogant statement. Yet in coming to Jesus, I found my earlier presuppositions were being challenged. As I read the Bible it talked about how Jesus was the only way to God. I read with interest verses about Jesus such as "I am the way and the truth and the life. No one comes to the Father except through me" (John 14:6, NIV). The Bible seemed to be pointing to the view that salvation was only through Jesus Christ and the work of the cross. Accepting this gift meant putting faith in Jesus, as highlighted in verses such as John 3:16: "For God so loved the world that he gave his one and only Son, that whoever believes in him shall not perish but have eternal life" (NIV).

At the time, I thought Christianity seemed to be taking somewhat of an egotistical position. What about those people who never came to know about the love of Jesus? Would they not receive eternal salvation? Clearly, coming to faith from a Hindu background left me asking so many questions, and these questions only intensified when a friend from a Pentecostal church asked if I had thought about being baptized. This was something that I was wholeheartedly committed to doing, but then there was that question of other religions that I needed to get my head round. Being baptized specifically into the name of Jesus and not just "God" made this question something that I could not avoid.

Many people would say to me it doesn't matter what religion you follow, as there is only one God. But then I would hear many new followers of Jesus say that they always believed in God, but it was through Jesus that He was finally made known to them. One Hindu shared with me how he had been searching but only when he encountered Jesus he stopped searching. And in Jesus I certainly felt I had arrived. Furthermore, in accepting Jesus I had received the Holy Spirit. My faith was built on experience. If God was real, we should be able to experience Him, and in Jesus I most certainly had an intimate relationship with Him. What's more, Christianity resonated with me as it was based on grace as opposed to works, the only religion like it. I knew I couldn't earn forgiveness, that no amount of trying was going to get me there, because I just knew deep down there wasn't much good in me. Grace could save me and change me, but without grace I was finished!

For the first few months after my decision to follow Jesus, I badgered God with questions about the different faith groups. The thing that finally swayed me to be baptized was that in Jesus I had a personal relationship with God. That word "personal" might be somewhat overused in Christian circles, and maybe we need to find new words lest overuse detracts from its utter significance. But it is true: in Jesus I had a *personal* relationship with God. He wasn't some distant deity and wanting to follow Him wasn't about performing a set of rituals each week to somehow attain to "Him" – though sadly for some that is all there is to their faith. It felt as if Jesus' disciple Peter was right when he professed that "Salvation is found in no one else, for there is no other name under heaven given to mankind by which we must be saved" (Acts 4:12, NIV) – no one but Jesus could open the way to an intimate relationship with God. No one else paid the price for my sin.

I realize that this perspective is not a popular one. But as I read the Bible I came to see that the God of the Bible was passionate for all to be saved. He had not come for one particular tribe or culture. Christianity wasn't just the arrogant Western religion I thought it to be in the past – Jesus Himself was from central Asia and I could see how people from across the world were encountering Him and finding life in Him. As I looked around me I discovered more and more people from other faith backgrounds encountering God through Jesus. I would hear stories of people experiencing

Jesus through visions and dreams, and people being miraculously healed when Christians prayed for them in the name of Jesus. The book of Revelation in the Bible gives a beautiful picture of what will one day be: "After this I looked, and there before me was a great multitude that no one could count, from every nation, tribe, people and language, standing before the throne ... They were wearing white robes and were holding palm branches in their hands" (Revelation 7:9, NIV).

Indeed, the God of the Bible was all-encompassing. He had made it simple; it was just a matter of turning our hearts to Him. This was a banquet to which everyone, good and bad, rich and poor, was invited by the King.

I had been warned that the week before my baptism would be difficult. And leading up to it I most certainly felt like I was caught in a spiritual battle. My friend had warned me that there was good and evil, and I was becoming increasingly aware that there had always been that tug. God had been calling me throughout my life and I had closed the door on Him several times, but I now realized that there was a third person in the equation – the devil was also vying for my soul. Interestingly, in many Christian circles there is little talk of the devil. I couldn't understand why, as the Bible mentions him from the beginning – he is deeply unpleasant but he can't be brushed under the carpet. Creation had started with the first humans in perfect relationship with each other and God, but that got distorted by the devil, and in a sense I, like everyone else, was being fought over my whole life. I had just been oblivious to it. I realized the fight had started many years earlier when I found myself rejecting God in favour of the temptations of this world.

The car journey to the baptism was hugely significant. Maria had been baptized by her grandfather in the Pentecostal church, but when he had passed away, her faith had fizzled out. I could understand why. Her grandfather had cared for her when her real father had disappeared, loving her as his own, and she knew it, meaning he was almost a priestly figure to her. As we were driving I talked to Maria about being re-baptized. Her faith had been dependent upon her natural grandfather and yet I felt God wanted her to know that *He* was her heavenly Father, that she was so deeply loved, and that He would never leave her or forsake her – there was a relationship for her to have directly with Him and not just through her grandfather. Maria was very reluctant to be baptized again. I knew that in some denominations you could only be baptized once. In others you could be baptized again if you had wandered away from the faith and wanted to recommit. Due to the sensitivity of the subject, I decided to drop the conversation and continued to pray for Maria on the journey to the church.

When we arrived, the New Testament Church of God in Lee in east London was packed. It was 22 June 2008. All these people had come to celebrate the commitments of several persons to God; many of them wouldn't have known the people being baptized, but the candidates for baptism were there because, like me, they had experienced the good news of Jesus. They were there because in Jesus we would become part of the family of God. Along with the others being baptized, I was dressed in white, symbolizing the cleansing of our sins in Jesus, and I listened with interest as one by one, men and women gave a short account of what their life was like before Jesus. These were stories of crime, despair, and pain before finding hope in Jesus. I saw grown people weep and celebrate their commitment to God.

It was an incredible feeling to go forward and to be given an opportunity to publicly share about how I had been messed up and God had given me a second chance. I wanted to shout from the rooftops because God had not forgotten me. There was no going back for me. I understood that for some, coming to faith in Jesus could lead to being ostracized by their families, and while I didn't have that concern, I knew many would not look favourably on my decision to follow Jesus. But in my heart I knew this was the right thing to do. I had encountered the grace of God. I had been on my way to death when Jesus intervened to offer me life; I was the prodigal son who had rebelled and squandered it all, only for God to welcome me back home. There was no going back for me now.

Under the stage was a baptismal pool. Some churches splash water over your head but in others it is done by full immersion. I knew it wouldn't have made a difference how I was baptized, as God would have accepted either. However, full immersion resonated with me. My sins were many and so it felt right to do it this way. It lasted for only a few seconds. Two people asked me if I was ready before baptizing me in the name of the Father, Son, and Holy Spirit. They leaned me back into the water, submerging me beneath it, and then raised me up. I had given my life to Jesus, and having done it, the overriding sensation I felt was a sense of God's pleasure. He was so very, very pleased! It was another milestone, and there would be many more to come, but at this particular moment He was utterly delighted that I hadn't shut the door on Him like I had done so many times before. It had been a long time coming, but I had finally arrived home.

At the end of all the baptisms, the church leader asked if there was anyone else who wanted to recommit their lives to Jesus. And then I suddenly saw Maria stand up and walk towards the pool. I was the impulsive one and this was totally out of Maria's character. Yet God had stirred her heart and this would mark a new phase of her faith journey. Sometime later, I asked Maria why she went forward and what the experience was like. She explained that she felt an overwhelming sense she was being called to go forward, similar to that feeling which I had had when I had given my life to Jesus some months before at Soul Survivor. Maria still vividly recalls the experience of being immersed in the baptismal pool, and the feeling of being reborn into a place where she felt so utterly loved. The baptism had lasted for just a few seconds, but in those brief moments she was able to let go of the hurt of losing her grandfather many years prior and to claim the love of her heavenly Father.

Maria and I had been married for a number of years and our wedding day had been a great celebration. Nonetheless, what had been missing was God. We had committed to each other without allowing God to be present in our relationship, and so for us, our being baptized on the same day was hugely important. As a couple, we had welcomed God into our lives and our marriage. We were no longer alone.

Having described something of life before I became a Christian, Maria wanted to share a little about how our marriage changed when God came into it – and into me!

After Ishaan was miraculously healed by God through Marci and Nick's prayers and discharged, we went to church to say "thank you" to them for their prayers. It was amazing to witness Manoj actually wanting to go to church. It was as if an invisible cord was attached to his heart, drawing him in. We followed Marci and Nick to Soul Survivor church where Manoj gave his life to God. That day I came home with a different husband … This was the beginning of a new Manoj. This new version said sorry, admitted when he was wrong, listened to me and loved me unconditionally.

It was so beautiful and touching when he asked to marry me again. This time it was going to be different. We privately had our vows reconfirmed in a church in 2012. There was no fanfare, no showboating; just us. Before, I knew I loved Manoj more than he loved me. I made my vows and knew I was going to have to accept this sadly. Now, I'm having to play catch-up in order to out-love him!

Our lives are a testament to the fact that life without God is bleak and empty. I for one do not want to go back there.

19

Surviving the Economic Crisis

In coming to faith, one area of challenge was my business. I regretted the way it had been built around speculation. I had been gambling on the market always going up and at its core it was wrong.

My business was about me making money, and what it failed to do was to adhere to Jesus' command to love others as yourself. I was caught up in a world in which everyone was looking out for themselves and I had forgotten that we were part of a community. But there was no immediate way out of this business. We had a pipeline of over 800 apartments that would come to completion over the next few years. I wanted out, but God was not about to wave a magic wand; He was going to ensure it would become a time of great learning.

PWC Accountants had a serious chat with me in May 2008 about my property business. Short of a miracle we were finished. Up and down the UK the construction industry had ground to a halt. Even sizeable developers like Barratt's and Taylor Wimpey had seen their share prices plummet. Property companies were going bust all over the country, particularly those which were trading in new-build homes, and many of ours were still only built on paper! The reality was that the developers needed their money from me to pay the banks the loans they had been given to build the new properties, but it would be difficult to get all my investors to complete on these properties with the mortgage market collapsing. I was stuck in the middle of a chain and the flow of cash that made it all tick was gone. PWC suggested I seriously consider administration.

I was so sorry to have taken so many crazy risks and built a business model that failed to reflect God's values. Not only would we lose huge amounts of money, but there were individual investors who were all caught up in the financial mess of it all. With no other option I began to pray. Often I would avoid spending too much time in the office because there was simply nothing I could do. And so I found myself regularly popping into a nearby church, falling to my knees and crying out for God's help. This would become my routine for the next twenty-four months.

I had not only overextended, but also given away personal guarantees. One senior accountant from a top firm had an off-the-record chat with me and asked if I had considered finding a way to take some money out. I said I couldn't because I was a follower of Jesus and it was against my principles. He impressed upon me to do something, if not for me then for the sake of my family. I was on the verge of losing not only my business but my home. But in having put my faith in Jesus, my security was no longer tied up in money. That is not to say I wasn't fearful of what might happen and the impact it would have on my family, but that I felt compelled to honour, love, and trust God first.

The impact on my health was more than evident. I constantly found myself having severe chest pains and anxiety attacks. On one occasion I had to come off the train because I was struggling to breathe. On other occasions I ended up in hospital because my whole body seized up. The attacks would happen suddenly, starting with a pins and needle sensation across my face, arms, and then my body. My chest would tighten and I would struggle to breathe or move. Over time I became accustomed to the attacks. I still suffer with anxiety today, though not at quite the same level. Despite all this, I still felt God was with me and carrying me through the storms.

During one particularly difficult month, I struggled to sleep. I felt like I was in a war zone, that there was some battle going on and prayer was the only answer to reaching a favourable decision with a particular property developer. One night during this period I had moved into my son's room to keep an eye on him as he was also poorly, and that night Maria woke up to see an angel in our bedroom. It was fully armoured, as if in battle. Maria wasn't afraid – she knew what it was and she quietly woke me up and told me to sleep in our bedroom while she took over looking after Ishaan. I slept well and was elated when the property developer I had been stressing over responded with a favourable compromise that week. Days later Maria explained about the angel. I was certainly in a battle and the outcome was very much dependent on praying for breakthroughs.

Over the course of the next few years I would see God intervene as I sat with one developer after another reaching compromises on cash settlements, or renegotiating contract prices so that our investors could complete directly with the developers. One developer suddenly decided to let me off and their banks asked him why he did it. He hadn't the faintest idea but had just felt he should. Another had put a claim into the courts to pursue me under the personal guarantees and then surprisingly did a U-turn. The impossible kept happening.

It is not over yet, and the business is still very fragile, but what it has all shown me is the power of prayer. It has been challenging, yet it has been good to be humbled by the experience.

As you can gather, the huge profit windfall we had been expecting in 2008 never came. Instead the company would make a huge loss and any value in the business would be completely wiped away. Nonetheless, God was in the midst of it all. He had chosen to navigate it through the worst, and the more I pondered on it the more I realized that God was interested in business. I had ruled out the idea of business on moral grounds, but God didn't seem to be rejecting the idea of business at all, if it was done by His values.

About this time I met Bridget Adams who, as I've mentioned, was a priest in the Church of England. With experience in the hi-tech business sector, she had worked up to director level and was surprised when God called her into ordained ministry, only to discover after training that God was not calling her into parish work but into priesthood in the business world. I met Bridget at a pivotal time when I was about to reject business for good.

Through Bridget I came across Bible passages confirming business as good. Indeed, the Bible highlighted the dangers of being wealthy with the account of a rich man who didn't make it after his death because of his meanness during his life. Yet there were also examples of good practice, such as the businesswoman in Proverbs 31 who is held up as a shining example of diligence, acumen, wealth creation, and charity. She ensures her trading is profitable but at the same time provides well for all her workers and "opens her arms to the poor and extends her hands to the needy" (Proverbs 31:20, NIV). I was learning that everything we have is His, and He expects us to use it well. Over the course of a number of months, I realized that God does not compartmentalize His creation. He is interested in everything! His presence fills everywhere; God was interested in my business, our businesses, but are we interested in having Him there?

I began to realize the power of business and how it could shape the world for good and for God. Shaping it for good would bring wealth creation in communities, with greater justice and relief from poverty for the world's poor, with the dignity of useful labour. Shaping it for God would bring "life in all its fullness" (John 10:10, NCV), a life reconnected with the One who made us and loves us, bringing hope, meaning, and purpose. I was amazed to hear of examples of Christians past and present who were making a difference to the world around them through business, and with Bridget Adams would eventually co-write a book entitled *Building the Kingdom Through Business* (Instant Apostle, 2012) for entrepreneurs seeking to set up godly businesses as catalysts for transformation – though, in truth, as with my TV series and plays with Maria, Bridget did most of the writing!

I was fascinated to hear of Christians being called into business, such as one missionary couple with a heart to help women out of prostitution. The women ended up in prostitution as they had no alternative; not only was it exploitation but an economic issue. Girls were being trafficked, some even sold by their parents. The solution would be an economic one, and so a business was set up to employ them, moving them away from slavery into freedom. And the women knew that it was Jesus who was setting them free. On one occasion, one lady who was trafficked at the age of thirteen suggested that they expand into a new area, but before even talking to the women about the jobs, she said, "So you want real freedom do you? You need to start praying to Jesus. He's the one who gives real freedom." The founder of the business said, "time and time again the women seem to understand more of Jesus than I do ... it's the little people, the poor, the unlovely and unloved that seem to have a greater understanding of who Jesus is and what He's about" (taken from my book *Building the Kingdom Through Business*).

It was slow coming, but meeting Bridget gradually opened my eyes to the potential of business to help change the world. Before I became a Christian, I had often looked at Georgina because she pointed to another world, a better world. And now I realized that business could do likewise. I had failed to see it. My vision had been so limited. Sometimes we need to be humbled to appreciate different perspectives, and sometimes we need to go through the mill to be refined. The experience of running my own business through the economic crisis and meeting Bridget had given me a new perspective. We were co-workers in God's service. God was not done with me yet.

I was about to finish this chapter here, but I paused and took a break. Standing on Watford High Street I bumped into a homeless man. It didn't seem like a chance meeting. He felt the same because he had only crossed over to get out of the shade. He told me how, despite his situation, God was standing with him and even enabling him to be a blessing to others. As he blessed others, God provided for his needs. He explained how he was even able to help a couple who had had their drinks spiked one evening by paying for their cab home, and he was able to do all this because of the love of Jesus. He ended by praying for me and sharing a verse from the Bible which he thought was relevant. It was in Galatians 6: "Let us not become weary in doing good, for at the proper time we will reap a harvest if we do not give up" (verse 9, NIV). I quote it because I strongly felt God had taken me outside to share his Heart for His vision of business. Fundamentally it wasn't about money. Yes, the money was important, and it would come, but primarily it was about doing good to others, and not tiring of doing it.

20

Instant Apostle

A fter meeting Bridget we began to write *Building the Kingdom Through Business*. Let me rephrase: she wrote it and I edited it. I didn't feel that my name had to be on the book because she was doing most of the work, but she was insistent that my name had to be on it and that God had said she was to write and I was to sift. Bridget was well known in the Watford area as someone who had committed to praying for the local Christian businesses. She would do this each Friday at 8 a.m. at a place called the Hub where a number of Christian businesses used to rent space and operate from. For five years she faithfully did this every week, and seeing her there and elsewhere I quickly noted how this woman spent a lot of time with God in prayer – so when she said God wanted my name on the book, I couldn't take it lightly.

Bridget wrote the book with great urgency and it was finished in about eight weeks. I recall mentioning the idea of submitting the book to some publishers, but she was quick to respond by saying that she felt God was calling us to set up our own publishing house.

This came totally out of the blue and I was swift to talk down the idea. I certainly hadn't felt anything of the sort. I knew very little about the publishing industry and had absolutely no desire to find out. And anyway, I already had enough stuff on my plate, such as getting my property company through the financial crisis. It was a definite "no" from my end. Ignoring Bridget, I proceeded to contact publishers about the book and she didn't mention the publishing idea again, which suited me fine. But about four weeks later I found myself having coffee with Bridget in a local café when the Holy Spirit suddenly impressed upon me that we were meant to start a publishing business after all.

It was a hugely profound moment that I distinctly recall. Not only can I tell you the name of the café we were in, but also where we were sitting and which chair I was sat on! There are many times I seek God on a particular dilemma and very often I don't get clear-cut answers and can feel a little left in limbo, not quite sure what to do other than go back to prayer, or be still and wait. But that day was extraordinary. The revelation came so powerfully: God had definitely spoken and now I had little choice but to embrace the new business venture.

Within weeks we had started work on setting up the new publishing house. Bridget prayed for the name of the company. I told her not to worry about it, but she was right – we needed the name to understand what we were about. She sought the answers to her questions and "Instant Apostle" was born. As the name suggests, we would be in the business of producing books and pamphlets much quicker than the industry standard, enabling writers to quickly comment on topical issues. For example, one biographical book recounted an ex-Page 3 model's experiences of the modelling world, promiscuity, and drug addiction, and our ability to release it to the market speedily meant she was able to lend her support to the Girl Guide campaign against Page 3. Similarly, in the case of another writer, we were able to release his book about living an audacious life and his role of heading up the anti-HS2 campaign at the same time as protestors lobbied against the new HS2 train link from Birmingham to London – his book covered this particular campaign and his influential role within it.

Having wrestled for months about whether business was inherently good at all, I now found myself putting into practice what our book was about – seeking to build God's kingdom through business. But unlike my previous commercial ventures, it hadn't started with the focus of profit. Rather, we had started with God's desire to see the world shaped for good. For years, I had engaged in business primarily to make myself money, and business had essentially been about lining my pockets. In contrast, Instant Apostle was about creating a better future and space for others to express their passions. Yes, of course business needed to be profitable and sustainable, but it had to be far more than that – it had to be about touching lives and bringing transformation.

It was evident from the start that this was a God initiative, that God was the CEO. It was His project and we were His co-workers. That is not to say that God didn't give us freedom to be creative and experiment, and that is what I love about God. He steers but He deliberately doesn't take over, allowing people to use the giftings He has given them. From the outset, God granted us great favour. I had mentioned to Bridget that if this was of God the books would come in without any work on our part, and within days new books began arriving, as well as the expertise we needed to take a book through the full publishing process.

In the early days of the publishing company, the life of W. T. Stead helped me to come to appreciate the purpose of Instant Apostle. W. T. Stead (1849–1912) was arguably one of the most important journalists of all time. He was certainly no saint, but he did lots of good, using journalism to challenge and speak truth at a time when newspapers contained little more than dry accounts of parliamentary debates. It was through his journalism that he was able to encourage the government to clear London's slums and give women equality. It would be some years after his death that some of his dreams for change would be realized. Nonetheless, he deserves to be commended for the part he played in bringing change. And in our very small way, Instant Apostle was seeking to do likewise.

One day I hope to find out about the true impact these books have had, but for now we enjoy the occasional story knowing full well that God likes to work quietly in the unseen places.

Instant Apostle had revolutionized my thinking about business. But it wasn't all plain sailing. Just because God was in it didn't mean that there wouldn't be challenges. I had come to understand quickly that when you tried to do good there would often be opposition. Bridget had already warned me about what to expect. "Are you absolutely sure, Manoj, that you want to be part of this venture?" she had asked. Rather naïvely I had said yes. After all, where else could I go when God was telling me to do it? There was just no point being outside of His will – I had spent enough years experiencing the consequences of that!

But I wasn't prepared for what would come. The day before the launch of the publishing house in a nearby bookshop, my son suddenly became extremely ill, suffering with a very high temperature and breathing difficulties. My wife and I did shifts that night, wondering if we might need to dash to the hospital. We kept giving him his asthma pump, and during the early hours he settled down; exhausted, I fell asleep with him. Sometime later, I woke up to the faint sound of my mobile ringing, and as I looked at the screen I saw "Doctor". I couldn't have accidentally pressed the phone to dial out as the phone was not near me. On seeing the word "Doctor" on the phone,

I immediately turned to my son. His breathing was extremely laboured and within a matter of minutes I was on my way to hospital, desperately praying for him to hang on. I distinctly remember the look on his face as I ran into the hospital, and I don't think I will ever forget it. The last time I saw that look was when he was in resuscitation in Northwick Park Hospital in 2008. Fortunately, Ishaan responded to a series of nebulizers. What would have happened if the phone hadn't woken me up? Would we have been too late? It seemed that God had come to our rescue again.

As for Bridget, she just about made it to the launch herself. She had recently become very sickly, and friends had borrowed a mobility scooter to help her get there. Convinced by God that Ishaan would be fine, I later left the hospital and managed to arrive in time for the last twenty minutes of the launch. It was great to see that Bridget had been able to make it as well, and in time I came to realize how important this was. God had initially spoken to her about Instant Apostle and she had been integral to setting it up, wrestling for the name of the company and its vision. But shortly after the launch Bridget passed away, having succumbed to cancer within just two months. Her time had come but she had finished well and had crossed into eternity. I was blessed to have known a woman with such a passion for Jesus, who was obedient to the end. Just a few days before passing away, she was still on fire for serving Jesus! I am amazed with what Bridget had managed to do in the last six months of her life. She had written a book and set up a new business, and all this despite her failing health. She had had cancer before and the doctors had given her the all clear, but when Bridget started falling ill again she mentioned that she wasn't afraid. She certainly knew where she was going, and her only concern was that she didn't want it to be painful. I am glad for her that the Lord responded to Bridget's desire and took her home so quickly.

Following the experiences of setting up Instant Apostle, Ephesians 6:12 in the Bible would take on deeper significance in my life: "For our struggle is not against flesh and blood, but against the rulers, against the authorities, against the powers of this dark world and against the spiritual forces of evil in the heavenly realms" (Ephesians 6:12, NIV).

Looking back, I now understand Bridget's urgency in writing the book and why my involvement in it was necessary. The baton had been passed on and it was now up to me to carry on her passion for business as mission. My property days were about gathering whereas Instant Apostle was about releasing. And clearly Instant Apostle was one area of my life where God was honing obedience – but, as ever, in a redeeming way. For although Instant Apostle is not in a position to pay me a salary at the moment, amazingly my property business is just stable enough to pay me to be able to do Instant Apostle. A business that was set up to make me rich is now literally paying for me to help others for free.

21

Taking Obedient Risks

One of the greatest struggles I found in becoming a follower of Jesus was obedience. Jesus most certainly modelled it well. In the Garden of Gethsemane, we see Jesus' heartfelt prayer to God the Father. He knows the cost of the pain that awaits Him in taking on the sin of the world and being nailed to a cross. Despite the prospect of what awaits Him, Jesus says, "Yet not as I will, but as you will" (Matthew 26:39, NIV). What I failed to realize when I committed to Jesus was that I too was signing up for obedience.

When I first came to faith in Jesus I was on fire for God. That sounds bad. I should still be on fire for Him! Nonetheless, it was a uniquely special time. I had just experienced light after being lost in the dark; I had been dead in my sins but now I was alive. I had been the lost sheep, but Jesus the great Shepherd had come to my rescue; I had been on my way to the pit of hell, but God had refused to give up on me. And with this new-found awe and wonder of the good news of Jesus Christ, I was certainly up for serving Him. Within weeks I had spoken to one of the pastors in my church about going for ordination in the Church of England. It was unusual to want to go for ordination so soon after becoming a Christian, but my mind was made up – I wanted to work for the church and I had already mapped it out. I would be in business for possibly a few years still, and during this time I could see a director of ordinands who would take me through a period of exploring what priesthood in the Church of England entailed. All being well, I would get to the BAP (Bishops' Advisory Panel) conference in about two years' time where a decision would be made on whether I was suitable for training.

I thoroughly enjoyed the process of reading books, shadowing vicars, and having great discussions with the director of ordinands, and this certainly felt like my destiny. Others exploring ordination would often comment on how they disliked the long process. In contrast, I relished the opportunity to explore. After all, wasn't this what I wanted to do? Before I knew it, the time to go to the BAP conference had arrived. I waited nervously for the decision and then finally the letter came through: I had not been accepted. I was devastated!

For weeks I questioned God. He knew how passionate I had been about serving Him, so why had He opted not to make a way for me to do so? It had not been a decision I had taken lightly. I knew that becoming a vicar would have meant a complete life change for both me and my family. I had been fully prepared to give my life for the sake of pastoring a church and its local community.

When the tirade eventually stopped and things were more settled, I began to realize it just wasn't God's will for me to get through. It had taken me the best part of two years to appreciate that relationship with God called for obedience, a turning away from my own plans to the plans He had for my life.

Interestingly, throughout my time of exploring ordination, one person challenged me to reconsider. He had felt that God may be calling me to serve the Asian community. I had rejected the idea but still had an inkling that God was in fact calling me to this work. One morning I decided that I really needed to know for sure, and I earnestly prayed for God to reveal His desire. It was one of those prayers genuinely asking God to have His way, when more often my prayers were ones of getting God to fulfil the desires of my heart as opposed to His. Within two hours of this heartfelt prayer, I found myself being invited to join the steering group of a new team in a Christian organization to support Asian Christians. I didn't want to do it but I had asked for a sign and boy, did it come. And so it was "no" to ordination but "yes" to serving the Asian community.

A few months later I moved on to working one day a week in the South Asian Forum team at the Evangelical Alliance. The hours were perfect, enabling me to still be able to concentrate on my business. And I began to find out why the work I was being called to was so important. As I looked around me I realized that the landscape in the UK and overseas was changing.

Christianity was moving from the West to the East as people in their multitudes were encountering Jesus in China, Korea, and South Asia. And as I looked around just my immediate connections, I was hearing stories of many Asians from other faith backgrounds choosing to follow Jesus. In the UK, many churches were seeing more Asians walking in asking deep spiritual questions. Recently, I was at a relative's house for a party and in the space of a few hours ended up having conversations about faith with a number of people, and later that evening I spoke to an Asian lady from a Hindu background who told me how she had become a follower of Jesus.

Clearly there was something spiritual happening amongst the Asian community, and the South Asian Forum was being called to play a small part in helping churches respond to the changes they were facing in terms of the ethnicities of their congregations. Where once the church was predominantly white English, churches were now seeing people from central Asia, East Asia, and South Asia interested in Jesus. Over the coming years, the Forum would facilitate the development of a booklet called *Jesus Through Asian Eyes* (The Good Book Company), answering key questions Asians have about Christianity. Many churches were ill-equipped to answer these questions, but now they had a simple resource they could give away and use for further discussion. Over time, the booklet developed into a full blown eight-week course called Discovering

Jesus Through Asian Eyes, giving churches the resource to have more in-depth discussions, should there be a need.

I had joined South Asian Forum out of obedience, and as I worked in this team along with others, I quickly came to realize that obedience was central to its calling. The booklet *Jesus Through Asian Eyes* didn't happen because we suddenly thought it would be a good idea. It came about because of a prayer meeting where there was a sense that God was calling the Forum to facilitate its development. The Discovering Jesus Through Asian Eyes course also came out of prayer. One of the writers of the *Jesus Through Asian Eyes* booklet was praying one morning about whether God was asking him to write a course, only to find someone contact him midway through, stating that he was using the *Jesus Through Asian Eyes* booklet with three Asian ladies and asking whether there was any course material to help him. The writer, as expected, was immediately convinced this was God's calling, and proceeded to work with the Forum in its development.

Interestingly, much of my life before Jesus involved risk-taking. I was naturally very impulsive and was quick to put ideas into practice. On one occasion I had met someone in the property field that was starting a company based around the idea of serviced apartments. At that one meeting, without any due diligence, I decided to give £100,000, only to find myself selling back my shares for £1 a year or so later.

Impulse had been my game. And yet, in becoming a follower of Jesus I suddenly found I couldn't act so impulsively. I discovered that obedience was a key aspect to following Jesus because obedience was key to God. And so the place of prayer would become integral to being obedient. As a rule, I have started to pray through all the big decisions I make. I know when I haven't prayed because I find myself going round in circles. Recently I put my house on the market to sell because my daughter had gotten a place in a school in a different borough. I had assumed we were meant to move. I stressed over the course of the next few months when no offers came through, and it was only after a long spell that I prayed and heard God saying, "I never told you to put it on the market in the first place." I could have avoided all the palaver of putting the property on the market and frantically cleaning it before each viewing if I had just stopped to pray and listen!

So, where did this leave the whole area of risk-taking? My earlier life had been based on the thrill of risks. Had obedience put an end to that? For a while I thought it had – that is, until I realized that God wasn't putting an end to risk at all. Over the course of time, I found that following Jesus was about blending risk with obedience. In terms of His plans, God seldom gave the whole picture. Sometimes He just gave a glimpse. With the *Jesus Through Asian Eyes* booklet there was a sense in the prayer meeting that God was calling us to develop this resource. We could have waited for further evidence that this was of God but the evidence only came much later, once we had started. We took the risk and it was through the process of doing it that we found God providing what we needed in terms of both financial and people resources. The whole process didn't come without its challenges, meaning that we had to continually stop and pray when hurdles came our way. The same happened with the development of the Discovering Jesus Through Asian Eyes course: although the writer was certain it was of God, it took risk to put it into action. It was months later that the financial needs would be met for launching a course of this nature in the UK and other nations. Someone once told me that another way of spelling "faith" was "r-i-s-k". When Bridget and I launched Instant Apostle it was done out of risk, as we didn't know much, if anything, about the publishing industry, yet faith helped to overcome hurdles. Faith meant taking a risk.

The key difference, I discovered, in understanding risk-taking as a follower of Jesus is that it is not done in isolation. It is not about going at it alone, but about working in partnership with a God who has given freedom, creativity, and responsibility. He has hired me as a co-partner. I get to have an opinion; I get to bring ideas to the table. We are in one team working for one cause. He isn't some dictatorial boss, but rather He is the CEO and I the managing director who meet at regular board meetings. There are spells when we seem to meet very regularly, and other times when it feels like He is on a sabbatical and has given me the reins. Sometimes I hear clearly, and sometimes I don't.

The thing is, God loves risk. He took a risk in making the world; He took a risk in giving stewardship to humans. Today He could quickly put right what humans have done wrong, but He chooses to work behind the scenes. We have created wars, polluted the atmosphere, exploited the poor, and done away with loving our neighbour as ourselves, and all this because we have done away with God. But that is the risk God took: He is a risk-taker. And yet, despite the mess we, as humans, have got ourselves in, we too are called to be risk-takers. Not risks for the thrill of it, not blind risks where we haven't calculated the cost, but risks in order to get whatever Jesus calls us to do, done. Playing it safe certainly isn't a biblical concept. Name me one Bible hero who played it safe.

As a follower of Jesus, I have come to realize that risk-taking is about helping to grow God's kingdom on earth. It is about seeking to do good and be a signpost to God in a world in which there is violence, selfishness, and lack of compassion. As people who have found hope, meaning, and purpose through Jesus, Christians are called to build a better world. This is a risky route because it is first and foremost about others before ourselves. But God will be with us on the front line and there is no better place to be. There is no doubt that existing in God brings the right kind of risk, should we be willing and obedient.

22

Transformed by
the Servant King

W riting this book has been a process of profound revelation. I now have a clearer idea of why I had certain experiences in my life and what these experiences were leading to. In becoming a follower of Jesus, I finally found the things I had been searching for, but not in the way I was expecting. Mr Thomas had encouraged passion, and this is certainly something I found in my relationship with God. Jorgen had encouraged me to strive for freedom, and in Jesus I have most certainly been set free from the consequence of sin, which is spiritual death. Kenya and family life had stirred a desire to be rich, and in Jesus I would discover infinite riches. Woven into my early life were the themes of passion, freedom, and money. These themes had become distorted until I met Jesus and He put a different spin on them. For so much of my life I had wanted to be filthy rich. And I am pleased to say that I finally am, not in monetary terms, but in Jesus. In Jesus, I am well and truly rich!

I see my journey of transformation as similar to that of Zacchaeus in the Bible. He was the chief tax collector, who abused his position to extract money from others. And yet one day when Jesus is walking through Jericho, He chooses to speak to Zacchaeus, of all people! These brief verses in the book of Luke speak volumes about what happens when one experiences Jesus:

> *Jesus entered Jericho and was passing through. A man was there by the name of Zacchaeus; he was a chief tax collector and was wealthy. He wanted to see who Jesus was, but because he was short he could not see over the crowd. So he ran ahead and climbed a sycamore-fig tree to see him, since Jesus was coming that way.*
>
> *When Jesus reached the spot, he looked up and said to him, "Zacchaeus, come down immediately. I must stay at your house today." So he came down at once and welcomed him gladly.*
>
> *All the people saw this and began to mutter, "He has gone to be the guest of a sinner."*
>
> *But Zacchaeus stood up and said to the Lord, "Look, Lord! Here and now I give half of my possessions to the poor, and if I have cheated anybody out of anything, I will pay back four times the amount."*
>
> *Jesus said to him, "Today salvation has come to this house, because this man, too, is a son of Abraham. For the Son of Man came to seek and to save the lost."*

Luke 19:1–10, NIV

Many of the religious leaders condemned Jesus for eating and associating with the "sinful". But that was

Jesus' specialty – He loved the sinners. That is the way of God, an upside-down kingdom where those you would least expect find mercy and favour. One touch from Jesus and Zacchaeus publicly accepts his sinful past and proceeds to put right what he has done wrong.

The reality is that there are countless people throughout the world experiencing the touch of Jesus and finding their lives turned upside down by this supernatural experience. In August 2014, I was at a church service where a Church of England vicar spoke about how a man experienced Jesus for the first time. The vicar recounted how he had met the man in a coffee shop. During the conversation it became clear that the man did not believe in the existence of God. The vicar moved on to state that often when he prayed, God would give him information about someone's life through words, an impression, or a picture. Over the course of the conversation, the vicar was able to pray for the man and give specific details about the man's life and relationship breakdown with his father. The man was utterly shocked and found himself in church the following Sunday giving his life to Jesus.

Reflecting on the story of this man's decision to follow Jesus, what is notable is that though he didn't believe in God, he was prepared to allow the vicar to pray for him. Like Zacchaeus, he became vulnerable. In my experience, God doesn't have a habit of forcing His way into people's lives. In the case of Zacchaeus, Jesus didn't simply barge into his life. Zacchaeus wanted to see Jesus, and that's why he climbed the tree. Something was stirring in Zacchaeus and Jesus responded. And it was the same for me too. In desperation I became vulnerable. In desperation I opened my heart, allowing Him to come in. I recall that moment when I gave my life to Jesus, walking into church as one man and leaving as another. Despite the changes that God has instilled in me, I still have a long way to go. I still have to pray against money temptations and sinful thoughts. I am still fallible and I hope that as you read this book you will be stirred to pray for me.

As you can imagine, my transformation in Jesus has led to countless conversations with people about faith. For some, doing religion is somewhat odd and out of touch. I often hear the view that "Well, if it brings happiness to you that is fine". In other words, "Don't try to convince me to engage with religion." For many, God is simply not relevant or simply does not exist. Why bother with God when you seem to be coping OK without Him? But there are equally as many people who are not living satisfied lives and are searching for freedom, a new life. Recently, I was walking home when one of my neighbours got chatting about her desire to encounter God. She was desperate to experience the divine, so then and there in the driveway we prayed that she would. Having opened her heart to God, I am sure He will come into her life.

As I discovered in my own spiritual walk, it is as simple as having a conversation. When I became a follower of Jesus, Georgina said, "Find a place, just you and God, and start talking." When I first started it seemed strange, like I was talking to myself. But that quickly changed. The more I did it, the more I started hearing from Him and feeling His presence in my life. I now have conversations with God in all kinds of places. The great thing is, He is always there, and starting out is so easy. You can tell Him your hurts, your joys, your concerns, your delights. You can talk to Him about the mundane and the profound. You can tell Him how sorry you are for the wrong you have done in your life. And don't let anyone tell you your sin is too great to be forgiven!

Lately, I was struck by the passage in the Bible where Jesus weeps over Jerusalem. He is making His triumphant entry into Jerusalem, and yet amidst the praising and rejoicing of many, Jesus weeps. This happened when He was coming down from the Mount of Olives, where He had a full view of the city. The fact that Jesus weeps when others are rejoicing at the recognition of His Kingship speaks volumes about God. Jesus weeps because He knows the consequences of Jerusalem at large rejecting Him. He says this as He draws near to the city: "Would that you, even you, had known on this day the things that make for peace!" (Luke 19:42, ESV) The nation is missing its moment. The messiah they had been waiting for has come to bring peace with God, and on the cross a few days later they will be offered forgiveness and life. But sadly, many miss this significant moment. God

Himself has intervened in history, God Himself has come as a man in their midst, but Jerusalem has missed it, has missed Him.

Since becoming a follower of Jesus, I too have carried the burden of seeing people miss their moment with Him. It hurts when I look at loved ones and no amount of explaining about Jesus makes any difference. In the pit of my stomach I ache with compassion, not because I am capable of such love, but only because Jesus lives in me and His love for them expresses itself. Because He weeps for them, I also weep for them. People often say, why do I share my faith, why not just let people be? I share because I have tasted the goodness and kindness of the living God. I share because I know what life is like outside of Him. I share because I want people to know life in all its fullness. I share because one day, when our time is up, I want to get to heaven and be elated with the people I see there. I share not to prove a point. I share because I have encountered a God who weeps and loves, a God who is broken by our rejection of Him, a God who sees people choosing to live outside of Him when He Himself made us all out of love and for relationship with Him.

As a youngster I could never get my head round the idea of the servant King. Why would the creator die for the created? I still don't get it, I still don't understand – but now I delight in the mystery of it all, rather than just being confused! It is so counter-intuitive for God to do something like that, yet such is the nature of the

Living God. At the Last Supper before His crucifixion, Jesus washed the disciples' feet. One of the disciples, Peter, was horrified by Jesus' act. This was the messiah who had come to save the world, washing his feet! Was this not insane – shouldn't Peter have been washing Jesus' feet? But Jesus explained that He had come to dust us off and clean us up. He hadn't come as the kings of His time, or the celebrities of today – He had come as the servant King. That is how God works. God serves. He served on the cross and He continues to serve, listening to our prayers when we need help. Who are we that warrant such attention?

23

True Happiness

In a sense, the focus of my whole life had been about searching for happiness. I was looking for contentment. I was searching for something to satisfy a deep internal longing and, looking at the world around us, this is clearly one of the key drivers in the lives for most people.

Evidently, my life in the world of property was about making money, but at its core it was ultimately about gaining happiness and hoping that money would bring me to that place of joy. The reality is it didn't. I am not saying money didn't make life more comfortable in certain respects. Of course it did! But it also brought a lot more stress and turmoil. In the book of Proverbs in the Bible, it says this: "Better a little with the fear of the Lord than great wealth with turmoil" (Proverbs 15:16, NIV).

This verse describes my life before Jesus very well. It was mayhem. The thing is, I had cottoned on to the fact I wasn't really fulfilled early in my business career, and I often used to look at Maria's mum and say I wanted what she had. At these points in my life

I should have done away with the love of money, and yet I stuck doggedly to the path I had chosen in the hope it would still somehow bring me to that place of satisfaction.

Most people would agree that we are all searching for happiness, whether that's through our careers, our relationships, getting drunk every weekend, living a promiscuous life, substance abuse, caring for our families – countless reasons good and bad. One way or another, we are on a journey and we want to arrive at that place where we can say we have finally made it, where we have come to the place where we are no longer searching.

After becoming a follower of Jesus, I came across a passage at the beginning of the Bible that stated that God made us in His image. I didn't really understand this until it was explained to me. Being made in the image of God means more than bearing traces of God; it means we were made for God, made to be in relationship with Him. If this is the case, could there possibly be any happiness outside of God? On this particular subject, C. S. Lewis, in his book *Mere Christianity*, said this:

> *A car is made to run on petrol, and it would not run properly on anything else. Now God designed the human machine to run on Himself. He Himself is the fuel our spirits were designed to burn, or the food our spirits were designed to feed on. There is no other. That is why it is just no good asking God to make us happy in our own way without bothering about religion. God cannot*

give us a happiness and peace apart from Himself,
because it is not there. There is no such thing.

In tracing my life before becoming a follower of Jesus, the happiest period was when I was at Cavina, my prep school in Kenya. And the reason for that was because during that time I was closer to God. At Cavina, God was fuelling my spirit, at Cavina I was in the presence of the Living God. But in moving on to secondary school I pushed God away and my level of happiness quickly disappeared. In many ways, my new life today in Jesus is pretty tough. There are many spiritual battles, and yet I am so much happier than I ever was outside of God. Happiness for me has come through being connected to God, and while some might argue that there is happiness outside of God, I simply don't believe it exists. I know this sounds like an arrogant statement, but if God is the source of everything good and we are made in His image, what is there outside of Him? The happiness I experienced before Jesus only existed because He made it possible. I was happy at the birth of my children, I was happy travelling, I was happy in many of my relationships. Before I became a follower of Jesus, I somewhat deluded myself into thinking that I was happy for many years. Of course, there were moments of happiness. But I say this to illustrate the point that I only really understood happiness when I met Jesus. When I invited Jesus into my life, all the great and wonderful things I had experienced paled into insignificance when compared to relationship with Him. It sounds rather harsh, but putting my life before Jesus and after Jesus side by side, there is no comparison. Knowing God is knowing joy.

Sadly, I wasted so much of my life outside of God being discontent. God had been chasing me throughout my life and yet I chose to ignore Him. I am sure we can all look at specific moments in our lives when we catch a glimpse of that other world, a signpost to another place where true happiness exists. Sometimes we see it in a person, or conversation, or while watching a TV programme and something resonates deep within, or when we see beautiful scenery that speaks to us of something more. God speaks in so many different ways through people and creation, and when He speaks He is often gently calling us back to Him.

In my case, God used a number of people to draw me to him of which Jorgen was one. While writing this book I came across an old address book with Jorgen's contact details. I was able to speak with his sister and was amazed to hear that it was his faith in Jesus that had carried him through the suffering of his terminal illness. I had often wondered what lay behind Jorgen's wonderful nature and life perspective but had been blind to it till now. Recently I had the chance to speak with Marianne Lindquist, Jorgen's mother, who relayed to me the extraordinary strengthening of his faith throughout his illness.

In 1992, Jorgen was diagnosed with a non-operable

tumour at the stem of his brain which sadly did not respond to chemotherapy. Following this, Jorgen asked to be taken to a Christian healing service, an experience which was to change his life. Although he was not physically healed, he had a spiritual encounter with Jesus and he then knew what he had been questioning for such a long time. Marianne told me that although his illness continued to progress, Jorgen always faced it without complaint. In December 1995, Jorgen's life came to an end and because of his amazing progression of faith he was never afraid of dying, saying 'I long to go home to be with my Lord'. Jorgen's story has made me realise that throughout my life God offered me so many chances at happiness, but I declined on every occasion and I can't get those years back.

When my son was ill, I cried out to God because deep down I knew He existed and only He could help me in my hour of need. I have heard countless stories of atheists refusing to believe in God, but when the rubber hits the road many have been known to fall to their knees in prayer because where else do you go but to the One you belong to? Ultimately we are made for relationship with God. He delights in us. Do we delight in Him?

I think for many of us, we believe that having God in our lives means missing out on the world we live in. But, as I discovered, following Jesus is not about escaping the world. It is quite the opposite. It is about living in the world and shaping it for good. Being a follower of Jesus is about the here and now and doing it with God. It is about allowing God into every area of our lives here on earth and going on the journey together. The great thing is that once we let God in, restoration is possible to ourselves, relationships, and the work we are called to do. Recently I had the pleasure of speaking to a gentleman who owns a Chinese restaurant. During the conversation I was reminded of my mother-in-law, Georgina. On the face of it she works in a large shop which pays her salary. But in having become a follower of Jesus, this is more than a job. It is the place where she can pray for the staff, it is the place where she can look after them and support them, it is the place she can bring joy to the customers, it is the place where the Holy Spirit will lead her to pray for people even if she meets them only once. And that is the difference inviting God into our lives makes.

One of the difficulties with gauging happiness is, how do you measure it? It is subjective and it swings like a pendulum. One moment can be happy, and the next something happens to scupper the joy. For many it is dependent on external influences, and yet because happiness is very much an internal thing, one's lack of happiness can easily be hidden. Not many people are up for confessing their unhappiness when they want to portray a totally different image of themselves. Most people would agree that being happy in modern life is somewhat challenging. The number of people suffering with depression is rising by the day and loneliness is a pandemic despite technology offering more ways of connecting with each other than ever.

Yet the happiness I have in Jesus doesn't waver in quite the same way. And the reason is simple. Happiness depends on faith. If we put our faith in the world we are putting our faith in something that will tarnish, rust, and pass away. But God doesn't pass away. Putting faith in God is putting faith in Someone everlasting. For many years God had been chasing me. He was always there, just like He is there waiting for you to respond as you read this book. If you haven't spoken to God before, why don't you start your conversation right now?

24

Legacy of Good Foundations

Reflecting on the impact our lives and actions can have on others, I wanted to end by sharing two things with you.

The first is a speech that Mr Massie-Blomfield delivered at Cavina School's Speech Day on 4 July 2014. It is a speech by a man who had a profound impact on my life when I studied at Cavina School all those years ago. It would be many years later that I would make a commitment to follow Jesus. Nonetheless, it all started in his school and I will forever be indebted to him. The second is a short talk given by a woman called Priya at a Jesus *satsang* (worship gathering). I had the privilege of meeting her some months earlier at a similar Jesus *satsang*. I had been invited that day to give a short talk and to share my story. I learned later that this was to play a small part in Priya choosing to follow Jesus.

It is fascinating how our past experiences can touch the lives of new people we encounter. Mr Massie-Blomfield had a huge impact on my life as a youngster and, because of what he invested in me, *I would one day be able to share my story with Priya who too would experience Jesus' love and begin to follow Him.*

Headmaster's Address,
Speech Day, 4 July 2014
Mr Massie-Blomfield, Cavina School

My thanks to my colleagues for all their hard work over the academic year just completed, as well as to the ground and maintenance staff, most of whom are here before 6 a.m. every day. My thanks, too, to you parents for entrusting your children to our care.

As you are aware, my son (who joined us at the beginning of the academic year) is relieving me of many of my duties, enabling me one day to "fold my tents like the Arabs and silently steal away". You may well ask, why do I delay? I admit I feel rather like King Canute trying to hold back the tide of advancing years. Yet it is precisely because I am of "a certain age" that I believe I still have something to contribute, and that is to endeavour to keep alive the Christian worldview that pertained [sic] when Cavina first opened her doors.

To many this must seem unrealistic. After all, we live in a post-Christian age where man is the measure of all things, and where God is a delusion – a useful prop for inadequate people like myself. It was not always thus. At one time Christian education was the norm, and Christ was seen as the beau ideal to which the young were expected to aspire. As a result they would seek to serve rather than to be served. Now such an approach is at odds with this thrustful modern age, and so many schools (and even churches) have chosen to move with the times. What we call Christianity is often only a veneer: scratch the surface and the wordling is exposed. Two days ago in morning assembly we sang George Matheson's well-known hymn written in the nineteenth century, the first verse of which is at odds with the spirit of our age. "Make me a captive, Lord, and then I shall be free: Force me to render up my sword, and I shall conqueror be." He continues in verse [four]: "My will is not my own till thou hast made it thine; if it would reach a monarch's throne, it must its crown resign."[1] Unrealistic? Undoubtedly. But just imagine the state of our nation if more of our political leaders had adopted that philosophy, and (like Paul) could state that they had been crucified to the world, and the world crucified to them.

The young boys and girls gathered here are the hope of the future. What are their ambitions? Do they want to make a difference? Do they dare to be different? Some of you may be familiar with H. G. Wells's short story *The Country of the Blind*. In case you haven't read it, allow me briefly to outline it: A lone climber, high up near the snow-covered peak of an unfamiliar mountain, was caught in a snowstorm. Continuing to climb, since he deemed it safer than to descend, he escaped the storm and was able to see a valley below him which appeared to be inhabited. In the last stages of exhaustion he managed to find refuge and was nursed back to health by the family who had rescued him. It was not long before he discovered that the people who dwelt in this valley were blind. Having fallen in love with the daughter of the house, he proposed and was accepted on one condition, that he should undergo a simple operation to remove his eyesight so that he would be able to take his place in the country of the blind and not be the odd one out. He was tempted to comply, but on the night before the operation, he slipped out of the house and returned to the land of the sighted.[2]

The analogy is fairly obvious. Your children are growing up to take their places in this fallen world – the country of the blind. If you doubt that then (with due respect) you are, in my opinion, in denial. Your children cannot opt out like the hero in H. G. Wells's story. Like us, they must serve their time in this country, the majority of whose citizens are spiritually blind. What will happen to them? Clearly there are only two possible outcomes: either they will allow themselves to be blinded for the sake of a spurious peace, or they will be used by God to open the eyes of the blind, enabling them to see the emptiness of their existence without Christ, and then see Him – who alone can turn their existence into a full and rewarding life. They, and all of us, must keep our eyes on Jesus, the author and finisher of our faith.

That is why my tents are not ready to be folded, and why I am not yet stealing away – silently or otherwise. For I want to play my part to ensure that your sons and daughters see Jesus more clearly; love Him more dearly; and follow Him more nearly. But I need your wholehearted support, and I pray that I can count on it.

1. "Make Me a Captive, Lord", George Matheson, 1892–1906.
2. H. G. Wells, *The Country of the Blind and Other Selected Stories,* London: Penguin Classics, 2007.

Mr Massie-Blomfield went on to say:

> Manoj attended Cavina School at a time when the majority of its pupils were drawn from several different faith communities. At that time, a parents' association existed for the sole purpose of supporting the school financially or otherwise. Unfortunately the committee was hijacked by a few radicals who were determined to dilute the school's Christian philosophy and direction.
>
> In this difficult time, when Cavina became headline news in one of our national dailies, Manoj was granted the opportunity to experience the truth of Jesus' statement: "I ... come [not] to bring peace, but a sword" [Matthew 10:34, NIV]. It is in such circumstances that faith is strengthened and I shall never forget the speech Manoj delivered as Head Boy during our prize-giving ceremony. He witnessed for Christ in ringing terms and told the audience, drawn largely from his own community, that Jesus, by His sacrifice on the cross, offered the pathway to God. Believe me, you could have heard a pin drop!
>
> Understandably, afterwards he was warned that if he chose to follow Christ he would find himself without friends or community support. This may have given him pause for thought.

Mr Massie-Blomfield was right: I did face some pressure. But what really withered away my enthusiastic faith was the desire to make money, as I have described.

Mr Massie-Blomfield concluded:

As I look back over my years at Cavina, Manoj stands out as an example of what happens when God's Word penetrates a receptive heart. It may take time to germinate, but it will eventually bear fruit, from which many will benefit.

Priya's Talk

I was born into a Jain family, the youngest of four siblings. My understanding of God was that He was one, and visible in so many different ways and forms to people. But as hard as I tried, I could not understand God – He seemed too distant and impossible to reach and the idea of meeting him one day, in a future life, was pretty difficult to fathom. But I tried my best to follow the religion that I knew and kept on failing and trying over and over again.

But then, three years and two months ago today. my life turned upside down. I lost my dear mum. My mum died, and I held God responsible and I held Him accountable ... How dare He take my mum away from me? How dare He not let her stay with me when I needed her? Why couldn't Mum be here to see me get my doctorate? Why couldn't she have been here for my graduation photo which she was so excited about? Why couldn't Mum be here to watch my daughter grow up? The sweet little girl she adored and spent most of her dying days looking after... why? I was angry and I hated God and I didn't want to know Him any more. I couldn't see how God could be good.

Nine months after Mum passed away we took her ashes to India, and this was followed by a short visit to Sri Lanka. On 11 April 2012 an earthquake occurred in the Indian Ocean. The 2004 earthquake had resulted in 10 metre waves in the resort we were staying in. I was terrified that the same would happen again. To cut a long story short, we ended up at the in-laws of the tour guide from the first part of our Sri Lanka trip. [While] there I was filled with rage, I think [this was the] last straw ... and [I] could not calm down. Moments later, I heard two voices in my heart. I just knew that a lady I had befriended called Julia was praying for me. At that moment I thought, wow ... I [had] given up on my God, but how strong must her faith be in her God that He was answering her prayers? I couldn't place the other voice, though. Months later, I found out that the other voice was Darshan Bhai's, a man who helped lead the Jesus *satsang* which Julia also went to. Here was someone who didn't even know me back then, but the Lord also carried his prayer to my heart. I can still remember the feeling that washed over me, the calm I felt, and that I wanted to believe in God as strongly as the two voices I heard did... There I was, broken, angry, full of hate, yet God was standing there all the time, I just didn't see Him. Little did I know what He had in store for me.

My story then moves to summer 2012. That September we started going to the Jesus *satsang* with Julia and Darshan Bhai on a regular basis. I was adamant that I had no desire to change faith. That I was only coming to socialize. But I felt comfortable taking my prayers to Jesus. And He answered... Time and time again He answered... And my faith in God was beginning to get restored... But still to me, it was all one and the same, just one God – believed in many different ways – and I was happy to just add Jesus to the list of gods I wanted to pray to. Because it was easier to do that than to risk losing the comfort and security of friends, family, and society. But the thing is, I wasn't quite happy, I wasn't satisfied, and I felt lost. Was I a follower of Christ? What did I want from God? More importantly, what did He want from me? And so I asked him, I prayed to God and asked Him that He would show me the path I should walk.

With time I found myself wanting to know more about this God. I wanted to believe, and I wanted to have faith. But I was scared. Because I was a sinner and I didn't see myself worthy of His love. Why would God choose me? Why would He care about me when most people don't? Why would He let me be a part of His family when I wasn't even prepared to admit to myself that I believed in Him? I was still incomplete, still lost, still searching... *Soon after, Manoj came to the Jesus satsang to share the story of how he came to follow Jesus.* And as I sat and listened, I knew that I wanted exactly what he had. I wanted to feel like that about God, I wanted to truly know God, to connect with Him. And so I prayed, and I asked God to show me the truth. And he did...

I know as I share this story, my spiritual brothers and sisters will be rejoicing for me. But I also cry. Because my family means everything to me and I didn't know how they would take my news, yet some of them are here today, supporting me and loving me, even though they may not understand why I want to follow Jesus. God's helping me rebuild relationships and showing me how to love others the way He loves me.

Through Jesus, God finally makes sense to me, I can take my prayers to Him, He is with me in my heart, and He gives me a peace that I cannot even begin to explain. He makes me want to be good, and do good. He helps me to turn away from sin. As a follower of Jesus, I no longer feel like I must plan every detail of my future, or spend my life worrying about every single minute detail. God's got all that covered and it's great to relinquish that control. I want to thank Him for letting me see the world through new eyes. I want to give Him glory for all the goodness in my world. And when I experience the lows, the frustrations, and sadness, and when I have to shed tears, I know that He is with me. I never ever have to be alone ever again because He walks with me. He never promised me a perfect now, but He does promise me a happily ever after, and I pray that all of you can know this promise too.

Last Page

I have pondered time and time again to find words that describe the nature of God as I know Him in the hope that this will draw people who do not know God closer to Him. I have racked my brains but I just don't think there are words in any human language that are able to describe the living God. There is a well-worn phrase that one has to find God for themselves. I guess it is true in this case. I am earnestly praying you will. If you would like to know more about following Jesus, or you want to ask further questions, you can do so by attending an Christianity Explored, Alpha, or Discovering Jesus Through Asian Eyes course. Such courses provide an opportunity to have friendly discussions and receive prayer. You can find out more by asking at your local church, or logging on to:

www.christianityexplored.org

www.alpha.org

www.discovering-jesus.com

If you have been impacted by this story, and would like an opportunity to commit your life to Jesus today, you might like to pray this prayer:

Dear Lord,

Thank You for all that You have done for me on the cross. I believe You are the Son of God who paid the price for my sins when You suffered there. I believe You died and rose from the dead. Forgive me for all the things I have said and done which have hurt You and other people. I accept You as my Lord. I am turning away from my sin. Please fill me with Your Holy Spirit so I can live for You from this moment onwards.

Thank You, Lord.
Amen.

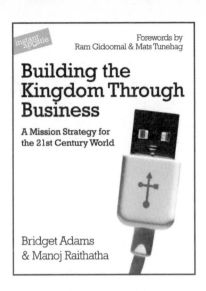

Building the Kingdom Through Business

A Mission Strategy for the 21st Century World

Bridget Adams and Manoj Raithatha

If it is business that shapes the world, then how can we use it to shape the world for good and for God? Against the background of an international debate on business ethics and more just societies, this book looks at Godly business in Biblical, historical, and practical ways. It includes advice on starting a business, and case studies of businesses already making a difference. There are lessons to be learned! And the world needs us to learn them. If you want to discover a new way of doing business then this book is for you. Whether you are a would-be entrepreneur, a church leader with a vision that mission can be different, or simply someone who wants to catch the new wave of what God is up to in the world of business, read this book and be inspired!

Published by Instant Apostle | ISBN 9780955913518